The Art and Background of Old English Poetry

Barbara C. Raw

Edward Arnold

© Barbara C. Raw 1978

First published 1978 by
Edward Arnold (Publishers) Ltd
25 Hill Street, London W1X 8LL

British Library Cataloguing in Publication Data

Raw, Barbara Catherine
    The art and background of Old English poetry.
    1. Anglo-Saxon poetry—History and criticism
    I. Title
    829'.1   PR201

    ISBN   0-7131-6100-0

Filmset in 'Monophoto' Baskerville 10 on 11 pt by
Richard Clay (The Chaucer Press) Ltd, Bungay, Suffolk
and printed in Great Britain by
Fletcher & Son Ltd, Norwich

Contents

Introduction

1   The manuscripts of Old English poetry: the material and its
limitations   1

Poets and poetry

2   The art of poetry   11
3   The poet and his audience   30
4   The poet and his world   45

Poetic art and form

5   Poetic form   65
6   Narrative method   82
7   Rhythm and style   97

Epilogue

8   Private poetry   123

Bibliography   133
Index   140

Unless otherwise indicated, all quotations from Old English poetry
are taken from *The Anglo-Saxon poetic records*, edited by G. P. Krapp
and E. van K. Dobbie (New York 1931–53), 6 volumes, by kind
permission of Columbia University Press.

Footnotes have been limited to specific references; books and articles which have influenced the work in a more general way are listed
in the Bibliography. The translations of the verse passages are intended to be literal rather than elegant; they are included simply as
an aid to readers with a limited knowledge of Old English.

Introduction

1 The manuscripts of Old English poetry: the material and its limitations

The only poetry which has survived from the six hundred years between the coming of the Anglo-Saxons in the mid-fifth century and their defeat by the Normans in the mid-eleventh is some 30,000 lines, considerably less than Chaucer's total output in verse. The main sources are four large manuscripts of the late Anglo-Saxon period: the Vercelli and Exeter books which date from the second half of the tenth century, the *Beowulf* manuscript from about the year 1000, and the Junius manuscript of the second quarter of the eleventh century.[1] A few isolated poems have been preserved in liturgical or historical manuscripts.

Of the four main manuscripts only one, the Junius manuscript, seems to have been written according to a coherent plan. The original design was for a lavishly illustrated copy of three Old Testament poems, *Genesis*, *Exodus* and *Daniel*, probably a presentation copy. The material in this first section of the manuscript, which includes the stories of the creation and fall of man, of Noah and Abraham, the crossing of the Red Sea and the saving of the three youths from the fiery furnace, corresponds very closely to the Breviary readings during Lent and to the prophecies read during the vigil service of Easter, and this suggests that the book may have been intended for reading during Lent. The poems are divided into fifty-six numbered sections, and if one section were read each day the material would last either from Septuagesima to the day before Palm Sunday or from Sexagesima to Holy Saturday. At some stage a fourth poem, called *Christ and Satan*, was added to the three Old Testament items by a different scribe and without any provision for illustration. This poem is unlikely to have formed part of the original scheme, but it must have been added at an early date because it contains an ornamental initial by an artist who worked on the illustrations to *Genesis*. It celebrates the triumph of Christ over the devil in his resurrection and ascension and would have

---

[1] For information on these manuscripts and on editions of the texts see Bibliography, Sections 1 and 2.

provided a fitting climax to a series of Lenten readings by adding material suited to the Easter period.

The Vercelli book, like the Junius manuscript, contains only religious literature: a collection of twenty-three homilies and six poems. Unlike the Junius manuscript, the first part of which is written with a regular number of lines to the page and with a uniform system of initials and section numbers, the Vercelli book shows considerable variation in spacing, in the use of headings and initial capitals, and even in the number of lines to the page, suggesting that the manuscript was copied over a period of time as suitable material came to hand. The contents are not arranged in any logical order and although the verse texts, two of which are saints' lives, are not inappropriate in a collection of homilies, they have no particular connection with the items which precede or follow them. It seems that the grouping of the texts indicates the sources from which they were taken. If this is so, then the first two verse texts, *Andreas* and *The fates of the apostles*, were probably already linked in the manuscript from which they were copied; of the other poems, *Soul and body I*, *Homiletic fragment I* and *The dream of the rood* were probably taken from a second source and *Elene*, which is placed apart from the other two groups of poems, from a third.

The Exeter book differs from the two manuscripts already mentioned in being a collection of both secular and religious poetry. In contrast to the other manuscripts of Old English poetry which contain a small number of fairly substantial poems, the Exeter book contains many very short poems. The manuscript opens with a group of fairly long religious works: the first three, known collectively as *Christ*, treat the three manifestations of Christ at his nativity, ascension and second coming; the other long poems are a life of St Juliana, two lives of St Guthlac, an allegorical poem on the phoenix, and a poem called *Azarias* which is close to parts of the poem *Daniel* in the Junius manuscript. The shorter poems include a number of descriptive and elegiac works—of which the best known are *The wanderer* and *The seafarer*—some gnomic poetry, several admonitory pieces and a collection of ninety-five riddles. It is thought that the collection may have belonged to Æthelweard, the patron of Ælfric.[2]

Most of the short secular poems which have survived are in the Exeter book, but the major secular works are scattered through several manuscripts. Chief among them is the *Beowulf* manuscript which contains in addition part of a biblical poem in heroic style (*Judith*), and three short prose works: *The marvels of the east*, the *Letter of Alexander to Aristotle* and a homily on St Christopher. The manuscript contains some coloured drawings illustrating *The marvels of the east*. Other important secular works are the six poems in the manu-

[2] *The wanderer* ed. T. P. Dunning and A. J. Bliss, pp. 1–2.

scripts of the *Anglo-Saxon Chronicle*, *The battle of Maldon*, the fragments of *The fight at Finnsburg* and *Waldere*, and the *Dialogue of Solomon and Saturn*. The manuscripts of *The fight at Finnsburg* and *The battle of Maldon* no longer survive: the former, which was at one time in the library at Lambeth Palace, is known only from an edition printed in 1705 by George Hickes, and the latter, which was destroyed in the fire in the Cotton library in 1731, is preserved in a copy made by John Elphinston in 1724, now in the Bodleian Library.

As can be seen from the fate of *The fight at Finnsburg* and *The battle of Maldon* manuscripts could disappear even as late as the eighteenth century; many more must have been lost through the dispersal of the monastic libraries in the sixteenth century, and even before this date the survival of manuscripts written in Old English, and particularly of verse manuscripts, was largely a matter of chance. Much Old English poetry probably existed only in oral form. There must, for instance, have been a large body of historical narrative which was never put into writing but which survived into the twelfth century to be used by Latin writers such as William of Malmesbury, who states that he obtained much of his information about the Anglo-Saxon kings from popular songs.[3] The lists of heroes in *Widsith* and the references in *Beowulf* and *Deor* to figures such as Weland, Sigemund and Eormanric give some indication of the wide range of pre-Christian heroic poetry which once existed; these poems too are unlikely to have been recorded for they were disapproved of by the church, which had a virtual monopoly of writing, but they continued to be recited even in monasteries. In about 797 the monks of Lindisfarne were rebuked by Alcuin for listening to tales of Ingeld instead of to the commentaries of the fathers; two hundred years later Dunstan of Canterbury was criticized for having learned the vain and frivolous songs of his heathen ancestors.[4] Religious poetry fared better, though even here much has been lost: Bede states that Cædmon composed a vast corpus of biblical poetry and Bede himself and Aldhelm of Malmesbury are said to have been accomplished composers of religious poetry in English, yet all that remains of this is the short hymn on the creation by Cædmon and the five lines of Bede's death song. Whereas much secular poetry failed to survive to modern times because it was never written down, religious poetry disappeared because the language and script in which it was written became unintelligible. The Exeter book, which was used at one time as a cutting-board, shows the hazards to which vernacular manuscripts were exposed, and there are many examples in mediaeval library catalogues of books which are de-

---

[3] For a full discussion of what poetry has been lost see R. M. Wilson, *The lost literature of mediaeval England*, chs. 1–3.
[4] *Monumenta Alcuiniana*, ed. P. Jaffé, p. 357; *Memorials of St Dunstan*, ed. W. Stubbs, Rolls Ser. 63, p. 11.

scribed as old, illegible and worthless, almost certainly because they were written in Old English and in insular script.[5]

The poems which have survived were composed at different periods and in different parts of the country, but these distinctions have been largely obscured because the poems have been transposed into a literary dialect—predominantly late-West-Saxon, though with some non-West-Saxon elements—which is common to all the manuscripts. In the Exeter book the language is so uniform as to suggest that when the poems were first assembled in the late ninth or early tenth century there was a deliberate regularization of the linguistic forms.[6] In the *Beowulf* and Vercelli manuscripts, on the other hand, the language varies from one item to another, allowing one to distinguish between those linguistic features which were introduced by the scribes and those which belong to an earlier stage in the transmission of the poems. *Elene*, for instance, shows some features which are characteristic of the Hatton copy of Alfred's translation of the *Cura pastoralis*, a manuscript which can be dated to between 890 and 897, and it can therefore be argued with some confidence that the poem has passed through an Alfredian copy.[7] Six hundred lines of the *Genesis* in the Junius manuscript can be shown on linguistic grounds to have been translated into Old English from an Old Saxon poem of the second quarter of the ninth century, fragments of which are preserved in a manuscript from Mainz, now in the Vatican library.[8] In *Beowulf* there are many lines where the metre requires the restoration of an early uncontracted form for the contracted form found in the manuscript, suggesting that a version of the poem may have been in existence as early as about 700, though it should be remembered that the traditional nature of poetry probably ensured the preservation of archaic forms long after they had disappeared from normal speech. In other cases poems can be dated on external evidence. *The battle of Maldon* must date from after 991 when the skirmish between the Danes and the English at Maldon took place. The late poem on the site of Durham must date from after 1104, when the relics of St Cuthbert were moved to the new cathedral, and from before 1109, because it is referred to in Symeon of Durham's *Historia Dunelmensis ecclesiae* which was completed in that year.[9] Most poems, however, can be dated only within very wide limits and even where a close connection can be shown between two poems, for instance *Beowulf* and *Exodus*, it is usually impossible to state with any certainty which was the earlier.

[5] N. Ker, *Catalogue of manuscripts containing Anglo-Saxon*, p. xlix.
[6] K. Sisam, *Studies in the history of Old English literature*, ch. 6, 'The Exeter book'.
[7] *Elene*, ed. P. Gradon, pp. 10–13.
[8] These lines are known as *Genesis B*, the rest of the poem as *Genesis A*.
[9] *Anglo-Saxon Poetic Records*, ed. G. P. Krapp and E. van K. Dobbie, vi, pp. xliv–v.

In appearance the manuscripts of Old English poetry differ enormously from modern poetic texts. They are invariably written in continuous lines, as though they were prose, and normally very little is provided in the way of punctuation or capital letters. In the Junius manuscript, which is more carefully written than the others, the half-lines of verse are marked by a point, and in some places a more elaborate system of punctuation, derived from that of liturgical manuscripts, indicates the inflections to be used when reading aloud.[10] In the Exeter and Vercelli books, on the other hand, the points vary considerably in frequency, and regular metrical punctuation is rare. The poems have no titles, and the divisions between poems are indicated simply by extra spacing and the use of large capital letters. In the Junius manuscript the three Old Testament poems are divided into numbered sections which are distinguished like the poems themselves by extra punctuation and large capitals. Since the numbers run in a continuous series through these three poems the division between them can be made only on the basis of the subject matter, though each poem does begin at the head of a fresh page. In the Vercelli book, where again both poems and sections of poems are marked by extra punctuation and large capitals, two poems, *The dream of the rood* and *The fates of the apostles* do not even begin on a new page: the second of these poems is divided from *Andreas* by only a single space instead of the more usual double one, raising the possibility that the scribe considered it to be the concluding part of this poem. In the Exeter book again the divisions between poems and between subsections of poems are not clearly differentiated, though there is a tendency to use more elaborate punctuation, double spacing and more extensive capitalization at the beginning and end of the longer poems than is used for short poems or sections of poems. Occasionally a poem ends with a word such as *finit* or *amen* to provide a clear indication of where the division comes. Such indications are found at the end of *Christ and Satan* in the Junius manuscript, *The fates of the apostles* and *Elene* in the Vercelli book, and *Christ I, The phoenix, Juliana, The seafarer, Vainglory* and *The partridge* in the Exeter book.

This lack of concern for visual boundaries between poems and for a visible distinction between verse and prose arose because the poems did not belong to a written but to an oral tradition. They are categorized as verse because of their strict rhythm and alliteration, not because they are set out on the page in short lines. No titles were needed, for the opening lines served to define their themes, and in many cases a conventional opening formula indicated clearly enough where a poem began in the manuscript. We know that some poems

[10] G. C. Thornley, 'The accents and points of MS Junius 11', *Trans. Phil. Soc.* (1954), pp. 178–205.

were composed while being recited while others were more probably
composed in writing, but in all cases there was the same emphasis on
the poem as something to be performed. In many cases poems must
also have been transmitted orally rather than in writing and this may
account for two striking features of the period: the lack of any record
of the authors of most of the poems, and the lack of any conception of
an authoritative text.

Many poems begin with a phrase such as *ic gefrægn*, 'I have heard',
or claim autobiographical status, yet in only three cases can poems be
attributed to a named poet. The nine-line *Hymn* composed at Whitby
about 680 by the poet Cædmon and the five lines known as *Bede's
death-song* are both preserved as part of prose narratives in which their
origin and authorship is described. Apart from these two short compositions, the only poems whose authorship is known are two in the
Vercelli book and two in the Exeter book. These four poems (*The fates
of the apostles, Elene, Christ II* and *Juliana*) all end with a passage where
the author, Cynewulf, has woven the initials of his name into the text
by using runic symbols whose names are essential to the meaning. His
purpose was not primarily to claim authorship, but to seek the
prayers of others for the safety of his soul, and it was probably for this
reason that he devised a form of signature which could not easily be
lost or changed.

> Her mæg findan   foreþances gleaw,
> se ðe hine lysteð   leoðgiddunga,
> hwa þas fitte fegde.   ᚠ [feoh] þær on ende standeþ,
> eorlas þæs on eorðan brucaþ.   Ne moton hie awa ætsomne,
> woruldwunigende;   ᚹ [wynn] sceal gedreosan,   100
> ᚢ [ur] on eðle,   æfter tohreosan
> læne lices frætewa,   efne swa ᚪ [lagu] toglideð.
> Þonne ᚻ [cen] ond ᚣ [yr]   cræftes neosað
> nihtes nearowe,   on him ᚾ [ned] ligeð,
> cyninges þeodom.   Nu ðu cunnon miht   105
> hwa on þam wordum wæs   werum oncyðig.
> Sie þæs gemyndig,   mann se ðe lufige
> þisses galdres begang,   þæt he geoce me
> ond frofre fricle.

Fates of the apostles 96–109

Here the man who is wise in thought and who takes pleasure in
poetry may discover who composed this song. F (wealth) stands at
the end: men enjoy it on earth. They cannot always keep it while
they live in this world; our joy (UW) on earth will turn to dust,
and then the fleeting ornaments of the body will vanish like water
(L) flowing away. When torch (C) and ink-horn (Y) pursue their
craft fearfully by night, hardship (N) will oppress them, the ser-

vice of the king. Now you can perceive who has been revealed to men in those words. May the man who receives pleasure from the course of this song remember to implore help and comfort for me.

At the end of *Juliana* Cynewulf completes his runic signature with an explicit plea to be remembered not simply as a poet but by his name:

> Bidde ic monna gehwone
> gumena cynnes, þe þis gied wræce,
> þæt he mec neodful bi noman minum 720
> gemyne modig, ond meotud bidde
> þæt me heofona helm helpe gefremme,
> meahta waldend, on þam miclan dæge.
>
> *Juliana* 718–23

I beg each man who recites this song, that in his pride he should remember me in my need by my name, and pray the judge that he, the guardian of the heavens and lord of power will grant me help on that great day.

For Cynewulf, the pleasure he had given through his compositions demanded a return in the form of prayers of intercession, something quite different from the material rewards expected by other poets. His demand for a continuing recompense rather than a once and for all payment implies that he believed that he had a permanent claim on his work. In general, however, poetry seems to have been considered as common property: each poet contributed to a continuing tradition, whether the telling of a story or the expression of an ideal; he modified the work of others and, presumably, expected his own work to be modified in turn.

A study of those few poems of which two texts survive shows that alterations were not confined to modernizing the language or to the removal of dialect forms.[11] Even in the poem *Soul and body*, where the Exeter and Vercelli texts are relatively close, there are changes in vocabulary and syntax, and in the case of *Azarias* and *Daniel* the differences are considerable. The two texts of *The dream of the rood*, the first in the Vercelli book, the second carved in runes on the edges of an eighth-century stone cross at Ruthwell in Dumfriesshire, are sufficiently close for it to be certain that they are versions of the same poem, but the exact relationship is unclear. It is likely that the Ruthwell inscription consists of extracts from a longer text for not only is it more concise than the corresponding sections of the Vercelli text: some lines are too short to scan correctly. There is no proof

---

[11] For a detailed comparison of some of these texts see Sisam, *Studies*, ch. 2, 'The authority of Old English poetical manuscripts'.

however that the text from which the extracts were made was a straightforward Northumbrian equivalent of the late-West-Saxon Vercelli text, nor is there any evidence that the opening and closing sections of the poem, which are not represented on the cross, existed at the time when the Ruthwell inscription was carved: the poem may well have been completely re-shaped in the ninth or tenth century. Cædmon's *Hymn* is particularly interesting in this respect. The seventeen copies of the poem, four in the Northumbrian dialect and thirteen in late-West-Saxon, show that already in the eighth century there were two quite different versions of the end of line five: *eordu bearnum* (LWS *eorðan bearnum*) and *aelda barnum* (LWS *ylda bearnum*). The first of these readings, which is unique to this poem, is probably the original, and the more familiar *aelda barnum* was probably substituted as a result of oral transmission of the poem.[12] In reciting a poem, even one with the authority which Cædmon's *Hymn* must have had, it would have been easy to forget a phrase and to replace it by some more familiar one which fitted the metre and alliteration.

The conditions under which Old English poetry has been preserved place special difficulties in the way of its interpretation. The first problem concerns the meaning of the poems in relation to the society which produced them. Our response to these poems depends partly on our understanding and experience as twentieth-century readers and partly on our appreciation of the meaning they had for their original audience: but whereas with later literature we usually know where, when, by and for whom a work was composed, in the case of Old English poetry we normally know none of these things. The poems are preserved only in the form in which they were known to copyists of the late tenth and early eleventh centuries, but many of them can be shown to have existed a hundred or more years earlier. The interpretation of the poems therefore depends on an understanding of their meaning both at the time when they were transcribed and the time when they were composed. But a further difficulty arises here, for we can date the poems only within very wide limits: to say, for instance, that *Beowulf* was composed during the eighth century is not very helpful, for the period includes both the Northumbria of Bede (d. 735) and the Mercia of Offa (d. 796) and the poem would be interpreted differently according to which choice one made. Moreover a poem like *Beowulf*, which treats the exploits of Scandinavian heroes of the late fifth and early sixth centuries, must derive from stories which had been handed down orally over a long period of time but we cannot get behind the written text to reconstruct an earlier oral version. The issue is not simply one of date but of environment. It has become fashionable to interpret *Beowulf* as a strongly Christian poem and to assume a high level of theological

[12] C. L. Wrenn, 'The poetry of Cædmon', *PBA* 32 (1946), pp. 277–95, especially 282–4.

knowledge in its original audience. This might be reasonable if we could be certain that the poem originated in a monastic environment of the kind which produced Bede, but although there is evidence that heroic songs were recited in monasteries there is no sign that Alcuin interpreted them as religious allegories. If we turn to a later period we find that there is evidence from the West Saxon royal genealogy and from a charter of the time of Athelstan for a knowledge of *Beowulf* or of something very close to it in court circles of the late ninth and early tenth centuries, but we cannot assume that a secular audience of this period, even after the educational efforts of Alfred, would have been as alert to religious symbolism as are some modern critics: they are far more likely to have been interested, as were Byrhtnoth's *comitatus*, in those things which were part of their daily life: loyalties and rewards, the winning of reputation, techniques of fighting and the ethics of the blood-feud.[13] The difficulty cannot be evaded by treating the poems without reference to their environment as though their words were all-sufficient, for the meaning of those words depends not only on their immediate context in a particular poem or in the poetry as a whole, but on the way in which they were used in the society to which the poems belonged.

The second problem concerns the criteria by which we evaluate the poems. We possess only part of the poetry of the Anglo-Saxon period, and we have no means of knowing whether what remains is a representative selection, for there is no evidence that the compilers of the anthologies did not simply copy what came to hand. There may have been several long heroic poems comparable to *Beowulf* or it may have been unique: we do not know. It is therefore impossible to talk of what is typical except in relation to what has been preserved, or to assert with any confidence that a poet is being original or innovatory. Moreover, our ideas on originality differ greatly from those we assume to have operated in the Anglo-Saxon period. The poems show that formulae—set phrases which conformed to the rhythmic pattern of the verse—played a major part in the composition of Old English poetry. Sometimes these phrases were used mechanically, but to a skilful poet they offered the possibility of unexpected variation of a kind impossible in poetry which had no traditional phraseology; because they were already part of the accepted language of poetry they drew a prepared response from the audience, and by using them in unfamiliar contexts the poet could deny this expectation and provoke new thought. This emphasis on the traditional, together with the

---

[13] For a recent discussion of these questions see E. John, '*Beowulf* and the margins of literacy', *Bull. John Rylands Univ. Lib.* 56 (1974), pp. 388–422 and the references given there, especially K. Sisam, 'Anglo-Saxon royal genealogies', *PBA* 39 (1953), pp. 287–348, especially 339–45, and R. Reynolds, 'An echo of *Beowulf* in Athelstan's charters of 931–933 A.D.?', *MÆ* 24 (1955), pp. 101–3.

assumption that poetry was a matter of craftsmanship rather than inspiration, is far removed from our modern approach. Attitudes to literary form were equally different from those to which we are accustomed. Many Old English poems seem shapeless to the modern reader, either because they have no well-defined ending or because of their digressive, encyclopaedic structure. There is good evidence that throughout the Middle Ages this gratuitous giving of information was welcomed, but it is still difficult for us to judge it.[14] We may assert after studying the extant poetry that the Anglo-Saxons liked digressions and that they preferred their poems to be written in an elaborately repetitive and formulaic style, but we are still left with the problem of how to evaluate poetry composed within conventions which are quite foreign to us: we cannot assume that something is good just because it was fashionable. Finally, our statements about the poems have to depend almost entirely on inferences from the text, and this means that we are forced to place tremendous pressure on it, scrutinizing each word in order to extract the maximum information from it. In so doing we tend to assume that the author and his original audience pondered the words equally intently. It is true that even when one is improvising one can still choose one's words, and even poets who never committed their work to writing must have tried out ideas and phrases in private before incorporating them in a recitation before an audience, but reflection is difficult for the listener who, unlike the reader, cannot halt the words while he considers them: there is no spoken text in the sense in which there is a written one. It is easy for the modern critic with his printed text and readily accessible works of reference to read too much into these poems. One must return here to the social context. In the hall, recitation must have been the chief form of entertainment, though reading aloud certainly occurred; a monastic community on the other hand encouraged private reading and meditation as well as reading in public.[15] The interpretation we give to each poem must depend, at least to some extent, on the context to which we assign it: there can be no one method of interpretation.

[14] G. Shepherd, 'The nature of alliterative poetry in late Medieval England', *PBA* 56 (1970), pp. 57–76.
[15] Alfred's mother read aloud to her children, see *Asser's Life of King Alfred*, ed. W. H. Stevenson, rev. D. Whitelock, ch. 23. For private reading in Benedictine houses see *Benedicti regula*, ed. R. Hanslik, *CSEL* 75 (1960), ch. 48, pp. 114–19.

Poets and poetry

2 The art of poetry

Poetry in the Anglo-Saxon period was not, as it is in some societies, a thing apart, its themes carefully distinguished from those appropriate to prose, its authors men of exceptional sensitivity and inspiration. Rather, it was the natural form of expression for material as diverse as the straightforward instruction of poems like *The seasons for fasting*, the proverbial wisdom of the gnomic poetry and the celebration of historic events in the *Chronicle* poems and *The battle of Maldon*. It was equally appropriate for public entertainment in the hall and for the intimacy of private prayer. For some, the art of poetry was a craft to be learned, and the professional poet, the *guma gilp-hlæden* of *Beowulf* for instance, or the much-travelled Widsith, was highly esteemed and lavishly rewarded. The ability to recite, however, and possibly too the ability to compose, was not confined to a specialized class but extended from the nobility down to the peasants. The remains of the six-stringed lyres found in the funeral deposits at Taplow and Sutton Hoo indicate that the kings and nobles of the seventh century counted music among their accomplishments,[1] and one of the most vivid accounts of courtly entertainment is the description of the old king, Hrothgar, telling stories of the past and playing the harp (*Beowulf* 2105–10). King Alfred is reported by Asser to have learned Saxon songs by heart and to have recommended the learning of them to his children, and the historian Bede was known to his contemporaries as an accomplished poet in the vernacular.[2] Bede's account of Cædmon reveals how widespread the ability to recite was.[3] The farm servants at Whitby abbey were apparently in the habit of entertaining themselves by reciting to the music of the harp; the cattle-herd, Cædmon, who had never learned any poetry, was so conscious of his inadequacy that he used to leave the house and go out to the cattle-

---

[1] R. Bruce-Mitford, *Aspects of Anglo-Saxon Archaeology*, ch. 7, 'The Sutton Hoo Lyre, *Beowulf* and the origins of the frame harp', pp. 188–97, and *The Sutton Hoo Ship-Burial*, I, p. 451.
[2] *Asser's Life of King Alfred*, ed. W. H. Stevenson, rev. D. Whitelock, chs. 22, 23, 75, 76; *The manuscripts of Cædmon's Hymn and Bede's Death Song*, ed. E. van K. Dobbie, p. 120.
[3] *Bede's Ecclesiastical History*, ed. B. Colgrave and R. A. B. Mynors, Bk. IV, ch. xxiv, pp. 414–21.

sheds when he saw the harp approaching him as it made its way round the company and each in turn was expected to recite to its music.

The same wide social spectrum is found among professional entertainers. On the one hand there are the poets such as Hrothgar's minstrel, distinguished figures who were probably permanent members of a court, and who were equal in rank to the members of the *duguð*; on the other were travelling minstrels, jugglers and acrobats, though little is known of this second group. There is a brief description in *The gifts of men* (82–4) of the entertainment provided by an acrobat, and the homilist Ælfric distinguishes between two kinds of entertainer: the *scop*, whom he equates with the Latin *poeta*, and the *gleoman*, a word he reserves for the Latin *mimus* or *scurra*.[4] The *Beowulf* poet had used the two words as synonyms but it seems clear that by the end of the Anglo-Saxon period the noun *gleoman* and the related verb *gliwian* had acquired a pejorative sense; the Canons of Edgar suggest this disreputable side of poetic entertainment when they state: 'We læraþ, ðæt ænig preost ne beo ealuscop, ne on ænige wisan gliwige.'[5] Two centuries earlier however, Aldhelm seems to have seen nothing wrong in acting the part of a minstrel, when he sang on the bridge at Malmesbury in order to attract an audience to whom he could preach.[6]

Apart from these few references, our knowledge about the profession of poet in the Anglo-Saxon period is derived almost entirely from the poetry itself. The gnomic poetry includes several references to singing, playing the harp, and composing poetry, among them a brief description of the minstrel, sitting at his lord's feet, his plectrum moving swiftly across the strings:

> Sum sceal mid hearpan   æt his hlafordes
> fotum sittan,   feoh þicgan,
> ond a snellice   snere wræstan,
> lætan scralletan   sceacol, se þe hleapeð,
> nægl neomegende.
>
> *Fortunes of men* 80–84

One shall sit with the harp at his lord's feet, receive treasure, and always swiftly twist the strings, let the leaping plectrum, creating harmony, sound loudly.

Two other poems indicate the poet's status. *Deor* is the lament of a minstrel who has lost the favour of his lord and been dispossessed of

---

[4] *Ælfrics Grammatik und Glossar*, ed. J. Zupitza, p. 302.
[5] *Ancient Laws and institutes of England*, ed. B. Thorpe, ii, p. 256.
[6] William of Malmesbury, *Gesta Pontificum*, ed. N. E. S. A. Hamilton, Rolls Ser. 52 (1870), p. 336.

the lands he once owned. *Widsith* tells of a poet who, although attached to a definite court, goes out to prove himself, rather as Beowulf does, visiting the tribes and heroes of Northern Europe and reciting and composing in return for gifts. The nature of these gifts reveals something of the relationship between lord and poet. Eormanric, whose court Widsith visits, gives him a ring; his own lord, on the other hand, gives him land; his ancestral estates:

> Ond ic wæs mid Eormanrice   ealle þrage,
> þær me Gotena cyning   gode dohte;
> se me beag forgeaf,   burgwarena fruma,   90
> on þam siex hund wæs   smætes goldes,
> gescyred sceatta   scillingrime;
> þone ic Eadgilse   on æht sealde,
> minum hleodryhtne,   þa ic to ham bicwom,
> leofum to leane,   þæs þe he me lond forgeaf,   95
> mines fæder eþel,   frea Myrginga.
>
> *Widsith* 88–96

And I was all the time with Eormanric, where the king of the Goths was generous to me with his wealth; the ruler of the city-dwellers gave me a ring in which was reckoned to be six hundred pieces of pure gold, counted in shillings; when I returned home I gave it to my lord and protector Eadgils as a reward for my dear lord because he, the ruler of the Myrgings, gave me land, my father's estates.

Like Beowulf, who gives Hygelac the gifts he had received from Hrothgar as a reward for his services in Denmark, Widsith gives Eadgils the ring he obtained from Eormanric. In both cases the motive is the same: the retainer gives to his lord not out of courtesy but precisely in return for the ancestral lands which are his due now that he has proved his worth.

The two classes of poet, the popular and the courtly, were united in the person of Cædmon, the first composer of vernacular religious poetry in England. The songs sung by his fellow servants were probably of a fairly popular kind. The miraculous gift Cædmon received in his old age was not his sudden and unexpected proficiency as a performer, for most of his companions could do as much, but his acquisition overnight and without visible tuition of the ability to express what he learned in the highly-ornamented language of the *scop*. Cædmon was believed to have been divinely inspired but it was his *cræft* or technical skill which testified to that inspiration and which, to judge from Bede's assertion that he was taught not by man but by God, was usually something which had to be consciously learned.

The West Saxon translation of Bede's account of Cædmon defines this poetic technique in two phrases: *geglenced* 'ornamented' and *wel geworht* 'well-wrought'. This working and ornamentation comprised three things: rhythm, syntax and vocabulary. Analysis of Old English poetry has shown that the metre was governed by very complex rules, though it is doubtful whether the poets or their listeners were fully conscious of them any more than we are aware of the equally complicated rules of grammar, word-order, stress and pitch which govern our everyday speech: it is a matter of instinct, resulting from long practice and imitation. There is no sharp division in Old English between prose and verse, but a gradation from ordinary prose, through rhythmic prose and loosely-organized verse to the highly-organized form of verse we classify as poetry. To this day, spoken English is strongly rhythmic, and it is likely that Old English, like modern English, contained a series of strongly-stressed syllables, each separated from the next by a variable number of lightly-stressed syllables which could be slurred together so that the strong stresses would come at fairly regular intervals. In poetic composition this underlying rhythm was formalized. Each line of verse contained four strong stresses, two in each half-line: the predominant rhythm, found in about fifty per cent of the half-lines, consisted of two strongly-stressed syllables, each followed by one or more lightly-stressed syllables, a pattern which fitted the strong root-stress which was normal in Germanic words; the strong stresses could be displaced forwards or backwards, giving five basic rhythmic types in all. Initial alliteration linked the third strongly-stressed syllable with one or both of the two stressed syllables in the first half-line, and further rules of length and grammatical and semantic rank governed the words on which stress could be placed.[7]

The proportion of lightly-stressed syllables in Old English poetry is much lower than it is in prose and this rhythmic feature is matched by a syntactic tightness, achieved by limiting the number of lightly-stressed parts of speech such as articles, pronouns and prepositions. The kinds of changes which were involved can be seen from a comparison of the poetic version of one of the metres of Boethius with the prose version from which it was adapted:

> Eala þu scippend heofones and eorþan, þu þe on þam ecan setle ricsast, þu þe on hrædum færelde þone heofon ymbhweorfest, and þa tunglu þu gedest þe gehyrsume, and þa sunnan þu gedest þæt heo mid heore beorhtan sciman þa þeostro adwæscð þære sweartan nihte. Swa deð eac se mona mid his blacan leohte þæt þa beorhtan steorran dunniað on þam heofone, ge eac hwilum þa

[7] For two rather different accounts of Old English verse rhythm see J. C. Pope, *The rhythm of Beowulf* and A. J. Bliss, *The metre of Beowulf*.

sunnan heore leohtes bereafaþ, þonne he betwux us and hire wyrð.[8]

Æala, ðu scippend scirra tungla,
hefones and eorðan! Ðu on heahsetle
ecum ricsast, and ðu ealne hræðe
hefon ymbhwearfest, and ðurh ðine halige miht
tunglu genedest þæt hi ðe to heráð. 5
Swylce seo sunne sweartra nihta
ðiostro adwæsceð ðurh ðine meht.
Blacum leohte beorhte steorran
mona gemetgað ðurh ðinra meahta sped,
hwilum eac þa sunnan sines bereafað 10
beorhtan leohtes, þonne hit gebyrigan mæg
þæt swa geneahsne nede weorðað.
Cotton Metres 4, 1–12

The structural unit in the prose passage is the clause, varying in length, and with anything from two to seven strongly-stressed syllables; the structure of the verse passage, on the other hand, is based on rhythmic rather than syntactic units, short two-stress phrases linked by alliteration. The more compact syntax, together with the change in rhythm, has been achieved largely by reducing the number of subordinate clauses and omitting as many as possible of the demonstrative and relative pronouns.

Also distinctive of Old English verse syntax are the constantly recurring structures such as prepositional phrases or combinations of two nouns, of which one is in the genitive case, which exactly fit a half-line of verse. A very common syntactic pattern in *Beowulf* is the combination of adjective, preposition and noun, as in the phrases: *geong in geardum, mærne be mæste, ænne ofer yðe, heah ofer heafod.* The adjective and noun are both of sufficient grammatical rank to take a strong stress and the preposition, together with the second syllable of the noun, provides the lightly-stressed syllables necessary to make up a half-line of Sievers's type A. This structure illustrates another of the constraints which operate in the inter-relationships of rhythm, syntax and alliteration. In the first 500 lines of *Beowulf* there are twelve examples of this type of structure in the first half-line and only one in the second; the probable explanation is that in a phrase of this kind both noun and adjective are of equal importance and must therefore both carry alliteration, something which was impossible in the second half-line, where only the first stressed syllable could alliterate. Another very common phrase-unit which similarly requires two al-

[8] Quoted from *King Alfred's Old English version of Boethius*, ed. W. J. Sedgefield, p. 10 = Latin i, met. 5.

literating syllables is the combination of two nouns or two adjectives linked by *and*. The first 500 lines of *Beowulf* offer twenty-four examples in the first half-line and only three in the second. In addition to having a distinctive rhythm and syntax Old English poetry was characterized by a special vocabulary. Many of these poetic words are compounds of words found singly in prose, for instance *beag-gyfa* 'ring-giver' or *brun-ecg* 'brown-edged'; some compounds such as *gold-wine* 'gold-friend' for 'lord' or *ban-fæt* 'bone-casket' for 'body' involve a metaphor, and it may be assumed that figurative language of this kind was considered appropriate to poetry. Other words such as *eafora* 'son', *gamol* 'old', *hæleþ* 'hero', *reced* 'hall' and *swegel* 'sky' are poetic synonyms for more ordinary words, and must have added to the ornate quality of the poetry, emphasizing its apartness from the prose of everyday life. It is noticeable that these words are never used in the elaborate rhythmic prose with which Ælfric and Wulfstan ornamented their preaching.

But despite this clear difference in vocabulary, the distinction between prose and verse seems to have been one of degree rather than of kind. Parts of the *Anglo-Saxon chronicle* are written in a rhythmic prose which stands out from the adjoining narrative, though it lacks the strict line-structure and alliteration of true verse; events of particular note such as Athelstan's victory at Brunanburh in 937 or the coronation and death of Edgar in 973 and 975 are recorded in regular lines of verse. The homilist Wulfstan embellished his sermons with passages written in a distinctive and highly rhetorical style characterized by sequences of alliterating two-stress phrases which resemble half-lines of verse.[9] Ælfric, who began by using these devices of alliteration and rhythm as an occasional means of enhancing the logical form of his sentences, later developed a kind of writing in which prose syntax and vocabulary were combined with regular rhythm and alliteration to form a kind of end-stopped verse, each clause corresponding to one line.[10] This elaborate rhythmic style was perhaps the English equivalent to the high style of Christian Latin writers described by St Augustine in his *De doctrina christiana*, a work which must have been familiar to English writers of the period of the monastic revival.[11] Whereas Classical rhetoricians had associated the different styles of writing with different kinds of subject, Christian writers, who considered all religious themes to be equally sublime, linked the three traditional levels of style—high, middle and low—with three different purposes: persuasion, judgment and instruction. A theory of style based in this way on authorial intention would account for the vary-

[9] A. McIntosh, 'Wulfstan's prose', *PBA* 35 (1949), pp. 109–42.
[10] *Homilies of Ælfric*, ed. J. C. Pope, EETS 259–60 (1967–8), I, pp. 105–36.
[11] E. Auerbach, *Literary language and its public*, pp. 33–9; B. F. Huppé, *Doctrine and poetry*; J. D. A. Ogilvy, *Books known to the English, 597–1066*, p. 84.

ing degrees of complexity in homiletic prose and in the religious poetry. The stylistic variations in the *Chronicle* and in the secular poetry, on the other hand, presuppose a classification of themes, each with its appropriate style.

Some indication of the literary forms and styles recognized by Anglo-Saxon poets can be gained from a study of the words they used in referring to poetry. The prose translation of Boethius's *Consolation of philosophy* marks the transition between prose and verse in the Latin original by phrases such as the following: 'Ða se wisdom ða þis spell asæd hæfde, þa ongan he eft giddian, and þus singende cwæð' and 'Ða se wisdom ða ðis lioð asungen hæfde, ða ongan he eft spellian and cwæð.' The prose passages are consistently identified by the noun *spell*, collocated with the verb *secgan*, while the usual word for the metres is the noun *leoð*, collocated with the verb *singan*; occasionally the nouns *gidd* or *sang* and the verbs *gliwian*, *galan* and *giddian* are used of the metres. The noun *spell*, which in the Boethius translation invariably refers to prose discourse, is used elsewhere of any narrative, whether in prose or verse. In *Beowulf* for instance the celebratory account of Beowulf's killing of Grendel, composed on the way back from the lake, is called a *spell* (873). The poet could have been thinking of a prose narrative, but the phrase *wordum wrixlan* suggests that it was in verse: the verb *wrixlan* 'exchange' is used of changing colours and it is likely that the phrase *wordum wrixlan* refers here to the technique of poetic variation rather than to an exchange of conversation, a meaning which is inappropriate in the context. The same concept of variation is found in the description of bird song in one of the riddles:

> Ic þurh muþ sprece   mongum reordum,
> wrencum singe,   wrixle geneahhe
> heafodwoþe.

Riddle 8 1–3

Through my mouth I speak with many tongues, modulate my song and often change my voice.

Another word which can be used of both prose and verse, though in the Boethius translation it refers only to verse, is *gidd* with the related verb *giddian*; its basic meaning is 'formal speech'. In *Beowulf* the noun *gidd* is used of the tales told of Grendel's depredations (151) suggesting that Hrothgar's humiliations may have been recorded in poetry; the verb *giddode* appears (630) as a synonym for *maðelode*, introducing the hero's speech to Wealhtheow in which he announces his intention of fighting Grendel, and in *Daniel giddian* is used of the warriors discussing the writing on the wall at Belshazzar's feast (727). The gnomic poetry categorizes the conversation of wise men in the phrase *giddum wrixlan* and the same association with wisdom is apparent in the lines in which the *gidd* is stated to be the attribute of the singer or poet:

> Wæra gehwylcum wislicu   word gerisað,
> gleomen gied   ond guman snyttro.
>
> *Maxims I* 165–6

Wise words are fitting for every man, the poem for the poet and wisdom for the man.

The use of the same word for poems and for formal speeches is of interest not only because it suggests the formal and ceremonious character of the poetry, but because two of the Old English lyric monologues, *The seafarer* and *The wife's lament*, are described by their poets as examples of the *gidd*. It is possible that this word referred to a specific literary genre, the speech of a fictitious character talking of the wisdom which springs from personal experience. A further characteristic of the *gidd* was its melancholy nature. The bereaved father of Beowulf's reminiscences (*Beowulf* 2446) utters a *gidd*, the sad tale of Finnsburg is both a *leoð* and a *gidd* (*Beowulf* 1159–60), and when Hrothgar entertains the company in Heorot he varies his recital with a *gidd* which is both true and sorrowful:

> Þær wæs gidd ond gleo.   Gomela Scilding,   2105
> felafricgende,   feorran rehte;
> hwilum hildedeor   hearpan wynne,
> gomenwudu grette,   hwilum gyd awræc
> soð ond sarlic,   hwilum syllic spell
> rehte æfter rihte   rumheort cyning.   2110
>
> *Beowulf* 2105–10

There was poetry and music; the wise old Scylding told stories from the distant past; sometimes the man brave in battle brought joyful music from the harp, sometimes he recited a true and sorrowful speech, sometimes the noble king told a wonderful tale in fitting manner.

The words *gidd ond gleo* suggest a contrast not only between speech and music but between what is sad and what is joyful, a contrast which is elaborated in the three phrases introduced by the word *hwilum*: the cheerful music of the harp, the true but sad *gidd* and the *spell*, or marvellous narrative.

In contrast to the *gidd* are the many references to the joys of music and poetry, expressed in the words *gleo* and *dream* and their compounds, such as *gleo-beam* 'harp', *gleo-cræft* 'art of poetry', and *gleo-*

dream. The word *dream* normally means 'joy' but it is used also of those
things which cause joy, in particular singing, and musical instruments
such as the harp and trumpet; the compound *gleo-dream* must therefore mean something like 'joy caused by music'. When, towards the
end of *Beowulf*, the poet wishes to convey the sadness of death the
metaphor he selects for the joys of this world is not the usual one of
the hall, but music:

> nu se herewisa   hleahtor alegde,
> gamen ond gleodream.

Beowulf 3020–21

now that the battle-leader has laid aside laughter, merriment and
the joy of music.

The emphasis on music raises the question of how poetry was performed. The distinction made in the Boethius translation between the
prose passages which were said and the metres which were sung
implies some difference, though it is possible that the verb *singan*
meant something closer to the modern 'recite' than to singing in the
musical sense. Clearly however some Old English poetry was sung.
Widsith gives a vivid picture of Eormanric's two minstrels singing and
playing together (103–8) and there are two references in *Beowulf* to
song and music combined, while Bede's account of Cædmon shows
that poetry was recited to the accompaniment of the harp. But it is
unlikely that this was so of all poetry. *The gifts of men* lists music and
poetry quite separately, implying that they were not invariably combined. Moreover the verb used of poetic performance is not always
the *singan* of the Boethius translation. The noun *spell*, unlike *leoð* and
sang is not collocated with the verb *singan* but with *secgan*, *reccean* and
wrecan, while the noun *gidd*, though occasionally collocated with *singan*, is more commonly found in company with the verb *wrecan*. This
raises the possibility that narrative poetry and perhaps also the lyric
monologue, were spoken not sung. If this is so, then Cynewulf, when
he says of the poet that he 'mæg eal fela singan ond secgan' (*Christ II*
666–7) is probably distinguishing between two kinds of performance
rather than merely varying his words.

The main purpose served by poetry was entertainment, and in this
the whole company could join, but it also had some more specialized
functions which gave the poet a distinctive role. The kings and heroes
described in Old English literature had an insatiable desire for fame,
and one reason for patronizing a minstrel was to ensure that one's
fame was recorded. In a passage at the end of *Widsith* this desire for a
good reputation on the part of the noble is linked with the reciprocal
need of the minstrel to find a generous lord:

> Swa scriþende   gesceapum hweorfað   135
> gleomen gumena   geond grunda fela,
> þearfe secgað,   þoncword sprecaþ,
> simle suð oþþe norð   sumne gemetað
> gydda gleawne,   geofum unhneawne,
> se þe fore duguþe wile   dom aræran,   140
> eorlscipe æfnan,   oþþæt eal scæceð,
> leoht ond lif somod;   lof se gewyrceð,
> hafað under heofonum   heahfæstne dom.
>
> *Widsith* 135–43

So the minstrels of men go wandering through many lands as events direct them; they speak of their need and give thanks; always, south or north, they find one wise in speech, generous in gifts, who wishes to increase his reputation before the tried warriors and to do what is noble, until everything departs, light and life together; he wins praise and a noble judgment in this world.

The word *lof* signifies the praise of one's fellow men, and *dom* their judgment on one's actions; the qualities which might merit such reputation are hinted at in the first part of the passage, in the references to wisdom and generosity. From other passages in the poem it is apparent that what was essential if one's reputation was to be anything other than local and short-lived was generosity to minstrels. Every time Widsith refers to himself it is to draw attention to the gifts he had received, and in his mention of Ealhhild he makes clear the close connection between gifts and the spreading of reputation:

> Ond me þa Ealhhild   oþerne forgeaf
> dryhtcwen duguþe,   dohtor Eadwines.
> Hyre lof lengde   geond londa fela,
> þonne ic be songe   secgan sceolde   100
> hwær ic under swegle   selast wisse
> goldhrodene cwen   giefe bryttian.
>
> *Widsith* 97–102

And then Ealhhild, the daughter of Eadwine, a queen renowned for courtesy, gave me another [ring]. Her praise spread through many lands when I had to relate in song where, under the sky, I knew for certain of a queen adorned with gold bestowing gifts.

It seems likely that a large body of verse once existed in praise of kings, though few traces now remain apart from the poems in the *Anglo-Saxon chronicle*. The *Beowulf* poet ends with a brief description of the praise accorded to the dead hero by his *comitatus*, which gives some indication of the nature of Old English eulogy, and epitomizes his heroes in the phrase, *þæt wæs god cyning*. The word *god* here does not mean 'good' in the religious sense but rather 'good for its purpose' and the phrase might be translated, 'he was a heroic king.'[12] Scyld, the ancestor of the Danes, is characterized as good because he reduced his neighbours to paying tribute, economically one of the best things a king could do (11). Hrothgar is described as good at the point when the Danes return from the monsters' lake, praising Beowulf and asserting that there was no greater hero nor one more worthy of a kingdom; the poet adds that in thus praising him they did not criticize their own lord, for Hrothgar too was a good king (863). Finally Beowulf himself is described in this way when he comes to the throne on the death of his cousin, Heardred (2390). This formulaic expression of approval is likely to have derived from encomiastic verse of the kind mentioned by Widsith. Another echo of this kind of verse can be found in Cædmon's *Hymn*. This poem was composed as Bede says *in herenesse Godes Scyppendes*, 'in praise of God the creator'; it was a religious equivalent to the praise of kings. The poem is often compared to the preface to the Mass which begins:

Vere dignum et iustum est, aequum et salutare, nos tibi semper et ubique gratias agere: Domine, sancte Pater, omnipotens aeterne Deus.

It is indeed right and fitting, our duty and our salvation that we should always and everywhere praise you, Lord, holy Father, almighty and eternal God.

There are of course similarities, but it is more likely that Cædmon, who certainly did not understand Latin, though he might have had the preface explained to him, was drawing on the language of heroic verse. His poem, in its West Saxon form, runs as follows:

Nu sculon herigean   heofonrices weard,
meotodes meahte   and his modgeþanc,
weorc wuldorfæder,   swa he wundra gehwæs,
ece drihten,   or onstealde.
He ærest sceop   eorðan bearnum   5
heofon to hrofe,   halig scyppend;
þa middangeard   moncynnes weard,
ece drihten,   æfter teode
firum foldan,   frea ælmihtig.

[12] M. Daunt, 'Some modes of Anglo-Saxon meaning', in *In memory of J. R. Firth*, pp. 66–78, especially 68–70.

Now we must praise the guardian of the kingdom of heaven, the power of the creator and his thought, the work of the glorious father, as he, the eternal Lord, established the beginning of every wonderful thing. He, the holy Creator, first shaped the heaven as a roof for the children of earth, and after that the guardian of mankind, the eternal Lord, the almighty Ruler, ornamented the earth for men.

The most striking feature of this poem is the accumulation of titles: six of the eighteen half-lines consist of them, while two others contain them. Only one of these titles is specifically Christian: *scyppend*, 'creator'. *Metod*, 'measurer', is a word which was used originally of the Germanic fates, but here it is appropriately transferred to God who measures man's fate and who, as creator, weighs the earth in his balance. The other three titles are derived from the terms habitually used of earthly kings. *Dryhten* and *frea* were used to express the two main relationships of the Germanic lord, the military one to his *comitatus* (*dryhten*) and the domestic one to his household (*frea*).[13] The last word, *weard*, 'guardian', is not restricted to human lords: in *Beowulf* it is used of the dragon, the guardian of the barrow, as well as of Hrothgar (921, 1390) and of Beowulf (2513). The best parallel to the *Hymn* is the phrase *rices weard* used by Beowulf when addressing Hrothgar (1390). In its elaborate sequence of titles the *Hymn* resembles the forms of courtly reference and address in *Beowulf*, for instance the opening of Wulfgar's speech to Beowulf:

> Ic þæs wine Deniga,
> frean Scildinga,   frinan wille,
> beaga bryttan,   swa þu bena eart,
> þeoden mærne,   ymb þinne sið.
>
> *Beowulf* 350–53

I will ask the friend of the Danes, lord of the Scyldings, giver of rings, famous ruler, about your visit as you request.

Another example of formal celebration is the poem *Widsith* itself, which glorifies the kings and heroes of Germanic antiquity, in addition to providing a kind of check-list of the tales a minstrel might have known. The three lists of kings, tribes and heroes which the poem incorporates conform to three formulaic patterns: *Ætla weold Hunum, Eormanric Gotum; Ic wæs mid Hunum ond mid Hreðgotum*, and *Heðcan sohte ic ond Beadecan ond Herelingas*. Each list is introduced by some eulogistic statement: the rulers are examples of those who intended their thrones to prosper, the tribes illustrate the virtue of liberality and the heroes

[13] D. H. Green, *The Carolingian lord*, ch. ix, pp. 270–321.

are all the best of comrades. In Icelandic the term for such a list was *þula*, a word which is related etymologically to the title given in *Beowulf* to one of Hrothgar's officials, Unferth the *þyle* (1165).[14] Unferth's precise status in unclear. He sits at the king's feet, a position often occupied by the *scop* or minstrel, yet he does not seem to be the same as the singer of tales. His title suggests that his task was to celebrate and record the past, but the comments on his behaviour by the poet and by Beowulf himself concern his courage and loyalty—or his lack of them—rather than his ability as poet or historian.

In recording the deeds of kings and heroes the poet offered fame and immortality in exchange for patronage, but he did more than this: he provided a model of behaviour for future generations. The comments in *Beowulf* and *The battle of Maldon* on the cowardice or loyalty of the members of the *comitatus* must have helped shape the attitudes of those who listened to these poems. Moreover there is evidence that men were influenced by the stories they heard: the Latin life of Guthlac of Crowland tells how he was stirred by the tales of his ancestors to take up arms, and it was the memory of the shameful deaths of these same ancestors that moved him to give up his warlike existence and become a hermit.[15] When the poets of the Anglo-Saxon period turned Latin saints' lives, including that of Guthlac, into heroic verse, using the language traditional to this genre, they did so not only because this was the established way of writing poetry but because by presenting Christianity in terms of spiritual warfare they could imply that the Christian hero was as worthy of imitation as his pagan predecessors. The author of one of the verse lives of St Guthlac in fact states that one reason for celebrating the deeds of the righteous was to provide an example which would be permanent because it was written down (*Guthlac* 526–9, 754–9), an interesting and bookish development of the pagan idea of fame, which was essentially transitory since it depended on the existence of speakers whose words would pass away just as the heroes they praised had done.

A further function of poetry was to preserve the wisdom of the past and to prophesy the future. When Beowulf returns home he describes to Hygelac the life at the Danish court and gives a picture of the old king playing the harp and telling stories of his youth and of the past (*Beowulf* 2105–14). Hrothgar is portrayed, as he is throughout the poem, as one who has gained wisdom through experience, and who expresses this accumulated wisdom through poetry. The close connection which existed in the Anglo-Saxon mind between music and wisdom can be seen in the gnomic verses, where singing is listed among the activities of the truly wise man:

[14] C. L. Wrenn, *A study of Old English literature*, p. 77.
[15] *Felix's Life of St Guthlac*, ed. B. Colgrave, chs. xvi and xviii, pp. 80–82.

> Ræd sceal mon secgan,   rune writan,
> leoþ gesingan,   lofes gearnian,
> dom areccan,   dæges onettan.
>
> *Maxims I* 138–40

It is a man's duty to give advice, to write secrets, to sing songs, to win praise, to give judgment, and to stir himself each day.

It is notable that Beowulf himself, though eloquent and accomplished, is never shown reciting or making music, and this seems to be connected with the contrast made in the poem between him and Hrothgar, the one celebrated even in old age for the youthful heroic virtue of strength, the other for the kingly virtue of wisdom. Music was probably already associated with wisdom in the pagan period, but the idea must have received an impetus from the fact that king David composed poetry and sang: pictures of David playing the harp and accompanied by his musicians are among the most frequently found illustrations in Anglo-Saxon manuscripts.[16] The idea that music and poetry were associated with wisdom also lay behind Cynewulf's justification of his vocation as poet. In his *Christ*, a poem celebrating the ascension, he talks of the gifts bestowed on man by Christ. The idea of Christ as a king handing out gifts is taken from the Epistle to the Ephesians (iv 7–12) but there the gifts are associated with the vocation of teaching. Cynewulf, however, identifies this grace and wisdom with poetry:

> Ða us geweorðade   se þas world gescop,
> godes gæstsunu,   ond us giefe sealde,   660
> uppe mid englum   ece staþelas,
> ond eac monigfealde   modes snyttru
> seow ond sette   geond sefan monna.
> Sumum wordlaþe   wise sendeð
> on his modes gemynd   þurh his muþes gæst,   665
> æðele ondgiet.   Se mæg eal fela
> singan ond secgan   þam bið snyttru cræft
> bifolen on ferðe.   Sum mæg fingrum wel
> hlude fore hæleþum   hearpan stirgan,
> gleobeam gretan.   670
>
> *Christ II* 659–70

---

[16] See for instance D. H. Wright, *The Vespasian Psalter*, EEMF 14, f. 30v, and two eleventh-century psalters: Cotton Tiberius C. vi, f. 30v, reproduced in F. Wormald, 'An English eleventh-century psalter with pictures', *Walpole Society* 38 (1962), pp. 1–13, pl. 27; and Cambridge Univ. Lib. Ff. 1. 23, f. 4v, reproduced in F. Wormald, *English drawings of the tenth and eleventh centuries*, pl. 20.

Then he who created this world, God's spiritual son, honoured us and gave us gifts, a lasting place on high among the angels, and also sowed and set in the mind of men many kinds of wisdom of heart. One he allows to remember wise poems, sends him a noble understanding, through the spirit of his mouth. The man whose mind has been given the art of wisdom can sing and say all kinds of things. Another can with his fingers skilfully and loudly set the harp in motion before heroes, touch the joyful wood.

Cynewulf appropriates this general claim of divine inspiration to himself in an autobiographical passage at the end of *Elene*, when he states that he, like Cædmon, received his skill in poetry direct from God (*Elene* 1242–50).[17] The same idea lies behind his association of poetry with prophecy. Cynewulf normally describes the prophets as singing (*singan*), though he also uses the nouns *gidd* and *leoð* (*Christ II* 633, *Elene* 342). There is not sufficient evidence to make it certain that this was the result of a deliberate choice, though it would certainly be in accordance with his conception of the dignity of the poet and of his vocation that he should consider the prophets as poets.

It is hardly surprising that if poetry was believed to come from God it was also considered to offer consolation in time of sadness. The belief that music could restore the sick to health did not originate with Christianity, but it was taken up by Christian writers and given a specifically Christian form. An early and influential example is found in Boethius's *Consolation of philosophy*. The Latin text of this work opens with a description of the imprisoned Boethius trying without success to console himself with the help of the Muses; Philosophy drives them from the room, asserting that they are making his sickness worse, and then gives him both comfort and renewal through her own songs. In King Alfred's translation into Old English the contrast between true and false consolation is accentuated by transforming Philosophy into Divine Wisdom, who drives out worldly sorrows and who later tells Boethius: 'Ac ic ongite ðæt ic þe hæbbe aðretne nu mid þy langan spelle, forðæm þe lyst nu leoða; ac onfoh hiora nu, forðæm hit is se læcedom and se drenc þe þu lange wilnodest, þæt ðu þy eð mæge þære lare onfon.'[18] Cynewulf may have been thinking of this curative property of poetry when he said that he drew the poem *The fates of the apostles* from his sick heart. A further development of this idea is found in the gnomic poetry:

---

[17] On the association between poetry and prophecy see G. Shepherd, 'The prophetic Cædmon', *RES NS* 5 (1954), pp. 113–22, and 'Scriptural poetry' in *Continuations and beginnings*, ed. E. G. Stanley, pp. 1–36, especially pp. 8–9.

[18] *Boethius*, ed. Sedgefield, p. 135, XXXIX, xii = Latin iv, pr. 6.

Longað þonne þy læs   þe him con leoþa worn,
oþþe mid hondum con   hearpan gretan;
hafaþ him his gliwes giefe,   þe him god sealde.

Maxims I 169–71

He longs less who knows many songs and can touch the harp with
his hands; he has the gift of his music which God gave him.

Because music and poetry played so large a part in the social life of
the Anglo-Saxons they came to be regarded, like feasting and the
giving and receiving of treasure, as symbolic of the good life as a
whole. In *Beowulf*, the court of Hrothgar is a place of almost perpetual music and singing: Beowulf tells Hygelac that the entertainment lasted all day. In the final part of the poem, by contrast, there
are no references to music, but only to its absence. In three places the
poet associates music with the inevitable passing of all that is good in
life. The first of these references comes in the description of the
solitary survivor who, as he places the treasure in the funeral barrow,
laments the ending of the society to which the weapons, armour and
precious cups had once belonged. He expresses his loss in terms of the
activities of that society: not the ceremonies of homage and treasure-
giving which are recalled in *The wanderer* but fighting, the polishing of
armour and drinking-cups, hawking, riding and music:

Næs hearpan wyn,
gomen gleobeames,   ne god hafoc
geond sæl swingeð,   ne se swifta mearh
burhstede beateð.   Bealocwealm hafað   2265
fela feorhcynna   forð onsended!

Beowulf 2262–6

There is no longer the joyful music of the harp, the entertainment
of the lyre, nor does the good hawk swing through the hall, nor
the swift horse stamp in the courtyard. Violent death has sent
many peoples from this world.

The second reference comes when Beowulf, recalling the death of
Herebeald at the hands of his brother Hæthcyn, compares their
father's grief to that of an old man whose son has been hanged, and
who walks lamenting through his empty rooms:

Gesyhð sorhcearig   on his suna bure   2455
winsele westne,   windge reste
reote berofene.   Ridend swefað,

hæleð in hoðman;   nis þær hearpan sweg,
gomen in geardum,   swylce ðær iu wæron.

Beowulf 2455–9

He gazes sadly at his son's room, at the deserted wine-hall, the resting-place of the winds, robbed of joy. The horsemen sleep, the heroes in the grave; there is no longer the music of the harp, merriment in the home, as once there was.

As in the previous passage, when death comes music ceases. The mention of music, which is specific to *Beowulf*, gives a quite different emphasis to these passages from that of the shorter elegiac poems. In *The seafarer* the decay of heroic society marks the old age of the world, when instead of man's rule men should seek the mercy of God, before whom the earth turns aside. In *The wanderer* the ruined civilization on which the speaker gazes is similarly the result of God's destructive power and again the wise man's recognition of the transience of wealth, friends and kinsmen, and of all the ceremony of the hall and of the *comitatus* leads him to abandon his hope of an earthly lord for trust in a heavenly one. The two passages from *Beowulf* in contrast make no mention of what one thinks of as the essential feature of heroic society, the relationship between lord and retainer: it is the riders who sleep in the grave, not the goldgivers and retainers of *The wanderer* and *The seafarer*. The sense of loss is much greater because there is no possibility of replacing these simple human activities by some equivalent in another world.[19]

The third passage in which the *Beowulf* poet talks of the absence of music is in the messenger's speech announcing the death of Beowulf and predicting war with both Swedes and Merovingians once the news is known:

ac sceal geomormod,   golde bereafod,
oft nalles æne   elland tredan,
nu se herewisa   hleahtor alegde,   3020
gamen ond gleodream.   Forðon sceall gar wesan
monig, morgenceald,   mundum bewunden,
hæfen on handa,   nalles hearpan sweg
wigend weccean,   ac se wonna hrefn
fus ofer fægum   fela reordian,   3025
earne secgan   hu him æt æte speow,
þenden he wið wulf   wæl reafode.

Beowulf 3018–27

[19] Strangely, the Anglo-Saxon heaven does not include the music of the harp, see below p. 29.

but sad of heart, deprived of gold, must tread a foreign land, not once but often, now that the battle-leader has laid aside laughter, joy and happiness. Therefore many a spear, cold in the morning, shall be raised up, grasped in the hands; the music of the harp shall not wake the warriors, but the black raven shall fly swiftly over the doomed men, relate many things, tell the eagle how he fared at the feasting while he competed with the wolf to rob the dead.

The main point of the passage is that Beowulf's death will result in war for his followers, but the idea is given a fresh emphasis. Beowulf's death is seen as a laying aside of one specific aspect of life. Instead of using the fairly common metaphor for death—walking out of the lighted hall into the darkness outside—the poet lists three of the pleasures of life in the hall: laughter, entertainment and music. The word *gamen* 'game' or 'sport' is often associated with music, for instance in the father's lament quoted above or in the compounds *gomenwudu* and *healgamen* in one of the descriptions of the entertainment at Hrothgar's court:

> Þær wæs sang ond sweg   samod ætgædere
> fore Healfdenes   hildewisan,
> gomenwudu greted,   gid oft wrecen,   1065
> ðonne healgamen   Hroþgares scop
> æfter medobence   mænan scolde.
>
> *Beowulf* 1063–67

There was song and music both together before Healfdene's battle-leader; the harp was touched, many lays were recited, when Hrothgar's minstrel had to entertain the company in the hall along the mead-bench.

The word *dream*, whose basic meaning is 'pleasure', is similarly associated with music in *Beowulf* 88. In later writings it came to mean a musical instrument (*Phoenix* 138) and in Alfred's translation of *The consolation of philosophy* the related words *dream-cræft* and *dreamere* are used of poetry.[20] Because Beowulf has relinquished this particular kind of happiness, the poet says, his followers must renounce the music of the harp, just as they must give up their ornaments on the death of their ring-giver.

In these three passages music symbolizes what is good and its absence what is bad. There is nothing overtly religious in the allusions, but there are other passages in *Beowulf* where music is given a specifically Christian meaning. Soon after Hrothgar has built Heorot the hall is attacked by a monster, Grendel. This creature, descended

[20] *Boethius*, ed. Sedgefield, p. 38, XVI, iii = Latin ii, pr. 6.

from Cain, outlawed by God and living on the boundaries of society, is understandably angry that his territory has been appropriated for the building of the hall, and that he, as an outcast, is excluded from the life in that hall. What particularly enrages him is the music of the harp and the singing of the minstrel, something which is hardly surprising when his normal habitat is the pandemonium of hell, *deofla gedræg*.[21] This contrast between the harmony of Heorot and the disharmony of Grendel's existence corresponds to a contrast constantly made in Old English religious poetry between the harmony of heaven and the disharmony of hell. In *Christ and Satan* heaven is filled with angels and saints who sing around the throne of Christ; the uproar in hell, the wailing and gnashing of teeth, can be heard twelve miles away (332–9). In Cynewulf's *Christ* (594) men are given the choice between joy in heaven or clamour in hell: 'swa mid dryhten dream, swa mid deoflum hream.' In *Guthlac* the devils who attack the saint shout war-cries while the angels who carry his soul to heaven sing a song of victory (264, 900, 1314–25). There is however one strange omission: the music of the Anglo-Saxon heaven is confined to the trumpets of the last judgment and the singing of the angels. Despite the efforts of Aldhelm to integrate minstrelsy and religion, or of Dunstan, whose harp was so well-instructed that on one occasion it played an antiphon of its own accord, Alcuin's relegation of the harpist to outer darkness seems to have prevailed.[22]

[21] The word *gedræg* appears twice in *Andreas* (43, 1555) as a poetic variant for *cirm* and *wop*; it is associated with the same two words in the description of the destruction of the world in *Christ III* (999); the general meaning is something like 'uproar'.

[22] See p. 3, n. 4, above and also *Memorials of St Dunstan*, ed. W. Stubbs, Rolls Ser. 63, pp. 21 and 63. The antiphon was 'Gaudent in caelis animae sanctorum qui Christi vestigia sunt secuti.'

3 The poet and his audience

Our knowledge of the audience for which a particular poem was intended, like our knowledge about the poets, comes largely from the poems themselves. Each poem which has been preserved, even though it may have passed through several different versions since it was first composed, is the work of a particular poet working at a particular time, and manifests a specific and individual relationship between poet, poem and audience. Some poems are explicitly addressed to an audience of one—for instance Cynewulf's ascension poem *Christ II*, *The order of the world*, and *An exhortation to Christian living*—and it is possible that they were intended for private reading; others, such as *Vainglory* and the two versions of the poem *Soul and body* address themselves to a more nebulous everyman figure. These two groups of poems were clearly intended for a more intimate audience than were some of the narrative poems with their assumption of public recitation. The poems of the *Anglo-Saxon chronicle* invariably begin, as do the prose annals, with the word *her* 'at this point', a form of opening which is found in no other group of poems, and which indicates that they were not considered as items to be performed separately but as chronicle entries in verse. The advent poems of *Christ I* presuppose some form of communal devotion whereas the poem *Resignation* and the *Prayer* of Cotton MS Julius A. ii and Lambeth Palace 427 belong with the many collections of private prayers. The opening lines of the *Maxims* of the Exeter book, which invite the audience to an exchange of wisdom with the poet, imply the possibility of a sharing of experience rather than the entertainment of the group by one man.

One very common convention involves the use of phrases such as *ic gefrægn*, *ic gehyrde*, *ic geseah* or *mine gefræge* which imply personal knowledge of the events described. Surprisingly, *The battle of Maldon*, which was composed shortly after the events it relates and which must have been based on personal knowledge, contains only one phrase of this kind:

> Gehyrde ic þæt Eadweard   anne sloge
> swiðe mid his swurde.
>
> *Battle of Maldon* 117–8

I heard that Edward struck one fiercely with his sword.

The other poems in which some authenticating phrase might have been expected are those in the *Anglo-Saxon chronicle* but again, apart from one example of *mine gefræge* in each of the two poems on Edgar, the poets claim no individual authority. *The battle of Brunanburh*, which at first sight appears purely heroic and oral in character, proclaims its literary and historical affiliations in the closing lines:

> Ne wearð wæl mare   65
> on þis eiglande   æfre gieta
> folces gefylled   beforan þissum
> sweordes ecgum,   þæs þe us secgað bec,
> ealde uðwitan,   siþþan eastan hider
> Engle and Seaxe   up becoman,   70
> ofer brad brimu.
>
> *Battle of Brunanburh* 65–71

Never yet in this island was greater slaughter done before on a nation with the edge of the sword, so books tell us, old historians, since the Angles and Saxons came here from the east over the wide sea.

It seems then that these superficially personal expressions are not related to actual knowledge but to poetic function and, in particular, to the relationship which the poet wished to create between himself, his story and his audience.

There was in Old English poetry a tension between tradition, of which the poet was the chief custodian, and individuality, the poet's personal contribution to tradition. When a poet uses phrases such as *we gefrunon* or *we gehyrdon* he appeals to the authority of an experience and a tradition which unite him with the audience, and establishes himself as one who shares with the audience a common past.[1] The poet of *Beowulf* for instance presents the early history of the Danish royal house as something which is well-known to all, material from the past which belongs to the common stock:

> Hwæt! We Gardena   in geardagum,
> þeodcyninga,   þrym gefrunon,
> hu ða æþelingas   ellen fremedon.
>
> *Beowulf* 1–3

Listen! we have heard of the glory of the kings of the people of the Spear-Danes in days gone by, how the princes did glorious deeds.

[1] For a slightly different treatment of these phrases see S. B. Greenfield, 'The authenticating voice in *Beowulf*', *ASE* 5 (1976), pp. 51–62.

His story, however, is concerned with particular events on which he can speak with an authority which derives from his individual knowledge, from traditions known to him alone, and which he is privileged to reveal to the audience. This individualizing technique appears very early in the poem, in the description of Scyld's funeral, where the poet claims that he had never heard of a more splendid treasure-ship than the one in which the king was buried (38). Again, when talking of the Danish royal house, he lists the three sons of Healfdene whose names were presumably well-known to the audience and then adds as a matter of personal knowledge that Healfdene's daughter had married the Swedish king, Onela (62). The building of Heorot by Hrothgar to celebrate his victory in war and his growing band of warriors is likewise mentioned by the poet as something of which he himself has heard (74). In five places the poet substitutes for the simple *ic gefrægn* or *ic gehyrde* either the negatives *ne gefrægn ic* and *ne hyrde ic* or a combination of these verbs with a superlative, in order to assert the excellence or uniqueness of what he describes, namely Scyld's funeral ship, Hrothgar's court, and the treasures given to Beowulf by Hrothgar and his queen (38, 1011, 1027, 1196, 1197). All these examples come in the first third of the poem, the Grendel episode; all assert the excellence of the Danish court. The superlative quality of the treasures given to Beowulf reflects honour not only on the hero but on Hrothgar and his queen: they fill their role, whose essence was generosity, to perfection, for they do not simply give, they give the best. The magnificence of Scyld's funeral is equally appropriate; he was after all a very great king, who had subdued all the lands around him before departing as mysteriously as he had come. Moreover the glorious funeral adds to the solemnity of the opening lines. But the very appropriateness of these allusions raises questions about the places where such phrases are not used. Beowulf's funeral at the end of the poem is not distinguished by any such phrase of excellence, nor are the twelve treasures given to Beowulf after the death of Grendel's mother; these last are not even listed (1867). The gifts presented to Hygelac and Hygd (2152–76), which are introduced by the phrase *hyrde ic* (2163), are the helmet, mailcoat, sword and standard presented by Hrothgar after the death of Grendel (1020–34), the necklace given by Wealhtheow (1195–1214) and seven of the eight horses given by Hrothgar (1035–45); presumably Beowulf retained the one with Hrothgar's saddle. These particular treasures are of great importance. The armour had belonged originally to Hrothgar's elder brother, Heorogar, who had predeceased him and who, for some reason not explained, had not wished to leave the wargear to his son, even though, as the poet says, he was loyal to him. Beowulf tells Hygelac that Hrothgar had specifically asked him to recount the lineage of these items. The objects are heirlooms; they give a sense of history and of ancestry to the poem. No other treasures could have equalled them and it would, therefore, have been an anticlimax to have praised the second gift. The reason why the poet does not claim that Beowulf's funeral surpassed all that he had experienced is rather different. Clearly this second funeral was no less splendid than the first. The pyre was hung with armour and weapons, the mound contained the whole of the dragon's hoard, the barrow was visible far and wide to travellers. But these splendours are predictable; any audience would know that Beowulf's end would outshine anything before or since. When the poet claims authoritative knowledge he is making his individual contribution to a story which was communal property. Like Hrothgar's minstrel he tells of things unknown to the majority of men (*Beowulf* 874–82). He claims to have heard of things which happened before the story of Beowulf began: the building of Heorot, the death of Ongentheow, the marriage of Onela, the funeral of Scyld, the reputation of Offa. He knows the details of the treasures, of the fight with Grendel and of the fight against the dragon, of the robbing of the hoard and of Beowulf's liability to break any sword he tried to use. He adds just that material which might be considered privileged information, and it is a mark of his realism that he gives no personal information on the underwater fight, of which there were no witnesses. If anyone asked how he knew these details, then he had been told. The tearing of the mead-benches from the sill of Heorot could have come to him through Beowulf's *comitatus*, the details of the dragon fight and the spoiling of the hoard from Wiglaf, the history of the treasures from those present in the halls of Hrothgar and Hygelac. But if anyone asked about the fight against Grendel's mother he could say nothing, for it would be too much to imply that his knowledge went back to Beowulf himself.

The pose chosen by the *Beowulf* poet then is one of authority based on exceptional knowledge about a common tradition. He asserts this authority by impressing his view of events on his audience, through a series of generalized reflections and comments on the action. Some of these general comments, like the gnomic poetry, state broad truths about the world. The most obvious example is the remark on the nature of dragons:

> He gesecean sceall
> hord on hrusan,   þær he hæðen gold
> waráð wintrum frod,   ne byð him wihte ðy sel.
>
> *Beowulf* 2275–7

He shall seek out the hoard in the earth, where, old in winters, he will watch over the heathen gold; he will be none the better for it.

More commonly these generalizations refer to human conduct, to universally accepted principles of behaviour. Quite near the beginning of the poem the poet comments, in connection with Beowulf the Dane, that a man should be generous in youth so that companions may stand by him in age. The statement that a man will prosper if he lives worthily is not inappropriate, though it is to some extent wasted on an insignificant character who merely fills the gap between Scyld, the marvellous ancestor of the Danes, and Healfdene, father of the Hrothgar who is ruling during the course of the story. It is important not as a comment on Beowulf the Dane but as a statement of the principle which will rule Beowulf the Geat, and which will be shown eventually to be untrue. Moral generalizations of this kind are particularly frequent in the third part of the poem, the dragon episode, where the audience is constantly reminded of the bonds of kinship, of the duties of the thane, of the contempt accorded to cowardice, of the dangers of avarice and of the inevitability of death. It is through these statements rather than through realistic description that the poet portrays the society in which his hero moves. Side by side with these passages are comments addressed more directly to the audience. After the description of Scyld's funeral the poet remarks that no one, whether a counsellor in the hall or a warrior in the field, knew what became of the ship. The lines emphasize the mystery of Scyld but they must also have struck the audience as a reference to the mystery of their own lives. The Cotton gnomes provide a more general application of the same idea:

>   Is seo forðgesceaft
> digol and dyrne;   drihten ana wat,
> nergende fæder.   Næni eft cymeð
> hider under hrofas,   þe þæt her for soð
> mannum secge   hwylc sy meotodes gesceaft,   65
> sigefolca gesetu,   þær he sylfa wunað.
>
> *Maxims II* 61–6

The future is dark and hidden; God alone knows, the father and saviour. No one returns here under the skies, who can truly tell men here about God's creation, the homes of the victorious people, where he himself lives.

The *Beowulf* poet's reflections on man's ignorance of the wanderings of evil spirits, and on God's careful providence are similarly related to the audience's experience, this time to their fears of the dark outside their halls, making the monsters of the poem seem more real to them. Often the poet comments directly on the action of the poem. He reassures the audience about the outcome of the fight with Grendel and warns them of the tragic end of the dragon fight; he draws attention to the moral and social implications of the action, for instance in his judgment on the feud pursued by Grendel's mother:

> Ne waes þæt gewrixle til,
> þæt hie on ba healfa   bicgan scoldon
> freonda feorum.

Beowulf 1304–6

That was not a good exchange which they had to pay for on both sides with the lives of friends.

He reveals the thoughts of his characters, attributing to Grendel and his mother, and even to the dragon, human emotions of fear, parental affection and resentment at injury which raise them above mere symbols of evil. He expresses surprise that Heorot withstood the fight and wonders at the way in which the giant sword melted in the monster's blood. Throughout the whole of *Beowulf* one is conscious, as in no other Old English poem, of the narrator's individual presentation of his story.

Whereas in *Beowulf* the poet distinguishes between the tradition which he shares with his audience and the details of that tradition which only he knows, in the biblical and religious poetry the distinction is between book-learning and tradition. Again, this is a poetic contrast rather than an indication of the poet's actual sources. The opening lines of *Exodus* and *Andreas* incorporate a variant of the *we gefrunon* formula found at the beginning of *Beowulf*. The poet of *Andreas* is probably borrowing directly from *Beowulf* as he does in a number of other places, most notably in his description of the ship (*Andreas* 360–62, *Beowulf* 38–40); the poet of *Exodus* however seems to be making independent use of what was a standard formula for beginning a poem. In choosing to introduce biblical or early Christian material by a formula associated with oral tradition these poets implied that the stories of Moses and of Andrew belonged to the audience in the same way as the story of Beowulf, that they were part of their common inheritance. In the same way the *scop* of *Widsith* claimed an equal familiarity with the peoples of biblical, classical and Germanic tradition, and the author of the West Saxon genealogy considered it appropriate to derive the West Saxon royal house from Noah.[2] The most striking example of this assimilation of book-learning and tradition is the poem *Daniel*, which is told entirely in terms of what the poet has learned or seen for himself. Not only does he introduce biblical material with the phrase *ic gefrægn* as though it

[2] Parker Chronicle, A.D. 855; see Sisam, 'Genealogies', pp. 320–21 and R. W. Chambers, *Beowulf: An introduction*, 3rd ed., pp. 202–3 and 317.

were derived from oral tradition instead of from books; at one point
he claims to have seen the events he relates:

> Þa geseah ic þa gedriht   in gedwolan hweorfan,
> Israhela cyn   unriht don,
> wommas wyrcean.

Daniel 22–24

Then I saw that company fall into error, the race of Israel acting
evilly and living sinfully.

The poet's assumption of the authority of an eye-witness is unique in
Old English narrative poetry, though it is the natural mode of presentation for the visionary material of *The dream of the rood*.
The poet of *Daniel* makes no reference to his real source, namely
books. The poets of *Genesis* and *Exodus* on the other hand contrast
what they have learned from books with what they know from hearsay. Much of the material in *Genesis* is marked by the phrases *þæs þe
bec cweðaþ* or *þæs þe us secgeað bec*, though the items singled out in this
way, apart from the reference to Lot's wife being changed into a
pillar of salt, are unremarkable and seem in no particular need of
authentication. When, at line 1960, the poet expands the Biblical
narrative with an account in heroic style of the battle of the kings
against Sodom, the capture of Abraham's nephew, Lot, and the pursuit by Abraham and his household, he signals both the stylistic
change and the change in source by the phrase *ic gefrægn* (1960, 2060),
emphasizing the heroic character of what follows. Whereas *Genesis*
consists of a fairly close paraphrase of the biblical text, with a few
major additions such as the descriptions of battles, *Exodus* is a poem in
heroic style which concentrates on the military aspects of the flight
from Egypt. Appropriately, therefore, the references to the authority
of books, which in *Genesis* were the norm, are confined in *Exodus* to
one passage, the speech of Moses after the crossing of the Rea Sea:

> Þanon Israhelum   ece rædas
> on merehwearfe   Moyses sægde,
> heahþungen wer,   halige spræce,
> deop ærende.   Dægword nemnað
> swa gyt werðeode,   on gewritum findað   520
> doma gehwilcne,   þara ðe him drihten bebead
> on þam siðfate   soðum wordum.

Exodus 516–22

After that Moses, the noble man, spoke to the Israelites on the sea-
shore eternal wisdom, holy words, a deep message. They call it

'day-word' as people still find in writings every judgment which God commanded them on that journey with true words.

The allusion is probably to the commandments set out in Deuteronomy, including the decalogue, but the point of the reference to books is that the homily on the transitoriness of worldly joy and the inevitability of judgment, a theme which develops from the lines just quoted, needed the support of an authority greater than the simple word of the poet.

A rather similar distinction is made by the author of *The phoenix*. In the first part of the poem, based on Lactantius's *Carmen de ave phoenice*, he presents the material as his personal discovery, the result of his questioning: he begins with the conventional *hæbbe ic gefrugnen* and, when talking of the tree in which the phoenix builds its nest (176), he again implies a knowledge based on hearsay. Later in the poem, however, when he develops the allegorical interpretation of the bird and of the tree, he calls on the authority of books (424, 655), at one point making a direct reference to the Book of Job as a guarantee of the truth of what he says (546-9). Yet the first part of his poem is as dependent on written sources as is the allegory. He is not concerned therefore to acknowledge his actual sources, but to give the weight of written authority to the moral implications of the story: the story itself needs no authority other than his own.

In some poems, however, there is an attempt to distinguish between different sources, more in the manner of a historian. *Guthlac B*, which draws on the Latin life by Felix of Crowland, refers to the evidence of books about Guthlac's life (878); the author of *Guthlac A* on the other hand not only calls on tradition, but makes it clear that the tradition is reliable because the events took place within living memory:

> Hwæt, we þissa wundra   gewitan sindon!
> Eall þas geeodon   in ussera
> tida timan.   Forþon þæs tweogan ne þearf
> ænig ofer eorðan   ælda cynnes.
>
> *Guthlac* 752-5

We are witnesses of these wonders. All these things took place in our own times. Therefore no man on earth need doubt it.

What is of interest here is the careful accuracy: these matters are common knowledge because they are recent. The kind of truth demanded by this poet is very different from that offered by the poet of *Daniel* or the poet of *Beowulf*. It is essentially a New Testament kind of truth, attested in the same way as St John's Gospel, by a genuine witness of events. The beginning of Cynewulf's *Elene* shows a similar precision. The poem opens with a statement placing the events in the two hundred and thirty-third year from the incarnation, the sixth year of Constantine's reign. There is no reference here to tradition, the distant past, hearsay or personal knowledge. The lines recall the careful dating in chapter ii of St Luke's Gospel, intended to establish that the story of Christ's birth was not mere myth but historical reality. Cynewulf may have taken the opening of the poem from his source, but even so, by retaining it he asserts the importance for his audience and for himself of the historical reality of the finding of the cross. When he tells the story of Juliana, a narrative which was equally derived from books, he begins with a formula which appears to be from a different tradition:

> Hwæt! We ðæt hyrdon   hæleð eahtian,
> deman dædhwate,   þætte in dagum gelamp
> Maximianes.

Juliana 1–3

We have heard heroes, bold judges, deliberate about what happened in the days of Maximian.

The implication is that the story has been passed down from one generation to another. Cynewulf, however, makes no attempt to exploit the tension between tradition and individual knowledge as the *Beowulf* poet does: for him the two were the same, for both were equally dependent on books. It may be therefore that the verb *hyran* does not imply indebtedness to oral tradition in Cynewulf's writings. Support for this view is found in *Elene* where the phrase *we ðæt hyrdon þurh halige bec* is used three times (364, 670, 852). This plural form of the verb, unlike the singular, appears only in religious poetry, and it is therefore possible that it has a different meaning from the apparently similar *we gefrugnon*, which is restricted to heroic contexts.

For Cynewulf, the authority of the written word was paramount. Except in his epilogues he makes little attempt to present his material in any personal way, and his conception of his role is always that of the man who makes known what he has learned from the writings of others. Other poets however, possibly with less learning or less self-confidence, found things harder. Whereas the secular poet had an established position as the custodian of the traditions and ideals of his people, the religious poet was in the position of a preacher who, unless he was ordained, lacked the authority to teach. As long as he confined himself to narrative he was secure, but the minute he offered instruction on religious matters he needed support from outside himself.

Some of the different ways in which poets solved this problem can be seen in the three poems known collectively as *Christ*. The first part of the *Christ* triad is a series of twelve meditations based largely on the antiphons sung at Vespers during the eight days before Christmas. There is no indication of the purpose these meditations served, though their syntax suggests that they were intended for some form of public devotion. The Latin antiphons on which the meditations are based follow a standard pattern. Each begins with a direct address to Christ under one of his Biblical or liturgical titles, or with an address to Jerusalem or to Mary; after a short elaboration of this title there is a closing petition which relates these particular attributes of Christ to the needs of the speaker. The following is typical:

> O Oriens, splendor lucis aeternae, et sol iustitiae; veni et illumina sedentes in tenebris et umbra mortis.

> O dawn of the east, brightness of the light eternal and sun of justice; come and give light to those who sit in darkness and in the shadow of death.

The Old English meditation on this theme (*Christ* 104–29) expands this brief address considerably. The reference to Christ as the rising sun is developed into a hymn praising his eternal sonship, perhaps through a play on the words *sunne* and *sunu*. The unfolding theme of sonship—the eternal birth of Christ from the Father and his birth in time from Mary, the two natures of Christ, the divine and human—is linked to the second theme, of the darkness of sin: the sinless light of the world comes to shine upon sinful man. In this passage, as in the poem as a whole, the phrases which in the Latin relate to mankind in general are assigned specifically to the speakers of the poem. For instance, where the Latin says simply: 'veni et educ vinctum de domo carceris, sedentem in tenebris et umbra mortis', the Old English identifies the prisoner with the immediate audience:

> We in carcerne 25
> sittað sorgende,   sunnan wenað,
> hwonne us liffrea   leoht ontyne,
> weorðe ussum mode   to mundboran,
> ond þæt tydre gewitt   tire bewinde,
> gedo usic þæs wyrðe,   þe he to wuldre forlet, 30
> þa we heanlice   hweorfan sceoldan
> to þis enge lond,   eðle bescyrede.

> *Christ* 25–32

We sit sorrowing in prison, await the sun, when the lord of life will
reveal the light to us, become the protector of our minds, and
surround our feeble wit with glory, make us worthy of the glory to
which he admitted us after we had been forced to turn despised to
this narrow country, deprived of our homeland.

The ideas are presented not as something offered by the poet to his
audience or even as part of a shared culture, but in terms of a shared
need. The poet never speaks in his own person, but always as one of a
group, and so the audience becomes identified with the sons and
daughters of Jerusalem addressed in the poem by Mary (89–91), or
with the Old Testament figures who have long sat in darkness (113–
18), or with those who await the harrowing of hell (154–9). In this
context the phrase *we gefrugnon*, used of the prophecy of Isaiah (301)
and of the wonder of the incarnation (78) expresses a complete unity
of poet and audience rather than the partial unity of the *Beowulf* poet.

In *Christ I* the poet is the spokesman for the yearnings of the group:
he speaks for them rather than to them. Cynewulf's ascension poem,
which forms the second part of the triad, works on a different principle. The poet presents himself as the man of authority, skilled in
book-learning, from whom the reader or listener is privileged to learn.
Although there is a plentiful use of the first person plural pronoun,
there is no sense that the poem is a communal object; it is Cynewulf's
poem. He may tell his audience that he and they, or he and one
other, are subject to the same forces, but there is always a separation:
when he says *we nu gehyrdan* (586) the implication is rather 'I have
just told you.' The role of the poet as teacher is established in the
opening lines, where Cynewulf invites the person he addresses to seek
the truth from him, and again in the epilogue, where he says *forþon ic
leofra gehwone læran wille* (815). This separation of poet and audience is
nowhere clearer than in the lines on the coming judgment:

        Is þam dome neah
þæt we gelice sceolon   leanum hleotan,
swa we widefeorh   weorcum hlodun
geond sidne grund.   Us secgað bec   785
hu æt ærestan   eadmod astag
in middangeard   mægna goldhord,
in fæmnan fæðm   freobearn godes,
halig of heahþu.   Huru ic wene me
ond eac ondræde   dom ðy reþran,   790
ðonne eft cymeð   engla þeoden,
þe ic ne heold teala   þæt me hælend min
on bocum bibead.

                                        Christ 782–93

It is now near the time of judgment when we shall be rewarded in accordance with our deeds throughout our life in this wide world. Books tell us that in the beginning the treasure-house of power, God's noble son, the holy one from on high, came humbly down to earth, into the maiden's womb. Truly I expect and also fear for myself a harder judgment when the lord of angels comes again, because I have not kept well what my saviour commanded me in books.

The third poem, that on the last judgment, shows yet a different approach. Much of the poem is told objectively, and it is only when Christ speaks to mankind at the judgment that the audience becomes involved in the poem. Cynewulf had talked of the judgment in relation to 'us', and specifically of its meaning for himself; this poet talks of it in relation to 'men'. It is only at the end that he changes from the third to the first person, when he urges his listeners to look into their souls before it is too late (1312, 1327). The full impact of the poem, however, comes in Christ's speeches, which belong in the poem to the day of judgment but which, because of the shift from the indefinite 'they' to the more immediate 'we', seem to be made direct to the audience of the poem. After a brief welcome to the blessed, based on Matthew xxv 34–40, Christ addresses the wicked. His words are derived partly from the same passage as the first speech, Matthew xxv 41–5, but this familiar homiletic theme of the reward due to acts of mercy done to one's fellow men is expanded by a long passage enumerating God's mercies to mankind in creating and redeeming him, and dwelling in detail on the pathos of Christ's life and, in particular, the sufferings he endured for man on the cross. This moving reproach is unlike anything in the sermon literature, though Wulfstan makes a brief reference to Christ showing his wounds and in another sermon stresses the need for man to repay Christ for his sufferings.[3] A better parallel however is the reproaches from the cross sung at the Good Friday service, and this comparison indicates the kind of dramatic effect the poem must have had.[4] Just as, in the liturgy, the congregation relives events from Biblical history, so in the poem the audience experiences the future judgment.

The different effects of Cynewulf's *Christ* and *Christ III* result from a shift in authority. Cynewulf's teaching is given in his own person, though it derives its force from books. The poet of *Christ III* teaches nothing himself; instead he adds to his impersonal though vivid account of the end of the world a scene in which Christ instructs man. A poem which exploits supernatural authority even more skilfully is *The dream of the rood*, where the poet withdraws from his real position, as

---

[3] *The homilies of Wulfstan*, ed. D. Bethurum, pp. 121 and 154.
[4] *Regularis Concordia*, ed. T. Symons, pp. 42–3.

the narrator of the dream, and becomes a character within the dream. In the first part of the poem, the description of the marvellous sign (4–27), the poet gradually moves into the vision and defines his position within it. He stations himself first as an imaginary observer:

> Þuhte me þæt ic gesawe   syllicre treow.

Dream of the rood 4

It seemed to me that I saw a wonderful tree.

The words are almost tentative: he claims no certainty for the vision at this point. But he is not alone in seeing the tree: it is watched by angels, by other men, by the whole of creation. The dreamer shares in this watch and so becomes a part of the dream, not merely a spectator of it. He is however a very humble participator: whereas the rest of the dream shines with a glory marred only by the change from jewelled to bloodstained cross, the dreamer is sinful, sorrowful and afraid. At this stage he assumes no particular credit or status for himself. Then the cross of the vision begins to speak. Just as the poet had watched the cross, so the cross watches the crucifixion. The 'I' of the poem now becomes not the poet but the cross which, having witnessed the crucifixion, can describe it in a way denied to the poet. The repeated phrases *geseah ic* and *ic beheold*, used first of the poet and then of the cross, increase the illusion that poet and cross are the same, and that the speech of the cross is addressed directly to the audience. This identification of cross and poet means that when the cross says in line 78, 'Nu ðu miht gehyran, hæleð min se leofa', the word *hæleð* appears to refer not to the dreamer but to the audience. The content of the speech which follows (78–94) shows that the poet is here impersonating the cross as he did in the description of the crucifixion, but the speech in which the cross commands the dreamer to reveal his dream to others (95–121) is phrased as though spoken by the dreamer. The poet here borrows the authority which belongs to the cross and uses it as though it were his own.

The dream of the rood is not the only poem to quote an authority beyond that of the poet: the *Precepts* of the Exeter book purport to be the instructions of a wise father to his son; *The wanderer* recounts the reflections of an imaginary solitary man and *Solomon and Saturn* describes a contest between two sages, overheard by the poet. In four poems—*The seafarer, Deor, Wulf and Eadwacer* and *The wife's lament*— the poet assumes a fictitious *persona*: what he says is, to quote *The seafarer*, 'a true story'; it is more real because it springs not from the wise men of the past, nor from some unidentifiable figure who told it to the poet or who was overheard by the poet, but from the poet's own experience, or rather from the experience of the person he claims to be. These poems, in contrast to those where the poet acts as a reporter, are without exception sad. Two, *Wulf and Eadwacer* and *The wife's lament*, tell of the sorrows of women separated from the man they love. *Deor* expresses a Boethian fortitude. The poet describes five examples of unhappiness from the past, each followed by the refrain, 'þæs ofereode, þisses swa mæg.' Unlike the speakers of *The wife's lament* and *Wulf and Eadwacer* who seem to emphasize their isolation from others, the speaker in *Deor* talks of misery in terms of a shared experience, well-known to all: of the love of Geat and Mæðhild he uses the formula associated with heroic poetry, *we gefrugnon*, and of Eormanric's tyranny the similar *we geascodan*; Theodoric's exile is characterized as known to many. The speaker's reference to his own loss of lands and patronage is placed within a context of universal experience, the constantly changing fortunes of this world, presided over by God. In *The seafarer* the conclusion that man should meditate on his true home which is in heaven, instead of placing his trust in the pleasures of this world, comes appropriately from a man who has chosen to give up a comfortable life on land and embark on a pilgrimage for the sake of God. In these poems the character appropriate to the teaching is one which is not too far from the poet's own to be acceptable. In *The dream of the rood* on the other hand the exhortation to honour the cross is one which requires more than human testimony: for the poet to impersonate the cross at the outset would seem conceit, but by his careful framing of the vision he combines a modest first appearance in his character of sinful dreamer, with the supernatural authority of the speaking cross.

Another poet who adopts a similarly modest approach, though for a very different purpose, is the author of *Widsith*. This poem consists of a long speech by the archetypal minstrel Widsith, with brief introductory and concluding passages which allow the poet to assume the character of the figure he portrays and to reinstate himself at the end. Whereas the poet of *The dream of the rood* uses the same pronoun, *ic*, for both himself and the cross, the poet of *Widsith* makes no overt attempt to identify himself with the speaker of the poem, and in this respect he is closer to the poet of *The wanderer* who merely reports what the solitary man said. But in both cases the audience would inevitably associate the fictional 'I' of the poem with the poet himself, and suspend all belief in him as anything other than the speaker of the poem. The manipulation of the audience in *Widsith* depends upon this identification of poet with fictional *scop*, for the implication of the poem is that the poet or reciter should be treated as was Widsith. As far as the relationship between author and audience is concerned the passages between the lists of kings and heroes are the most interesting, though they are not the ostensible reason for the poem. Widsith's speech begins with the assertion that those who wish to prosper must

live fittingly, a general statement of fact, introduced by the verb *sceal*
to indicate something which is an inherent or essential quality (11–
13); the appeal here is to the universal as it is in the gnomic poetry or in
the general comments of *Beowulf*. The prologue to the second list appeals
to personal experience rather than general principle (50–56). The
poet has put to the test both good and evil; he is a man of experience,
in particular the experience of exile, far from his kinsmen. In choosing
this particular form of deprivation the poet can exploit the sympathy
which the exile invariably aroused: Widsith is by no means unique.
Yet he is unique in one respect, for his exile was not one of poverty
and loneliness: wherever he went he found generous patrons. A further reminder of this generosity comes in the interlude between the
second and third lists, where he describes the gifts he received from
Eormanric and his queen and from his own lord, Eadgils (88–98). It
is at this point that the poet draws attention, in an oblique way, to the
implications of these references to generosity, by a direct reference to
Widsith's reputation: when he praised Ealhhild's liberality, thus
ensuring that her fame would spread through many lands, all who
heard him, men who were good judges of the matter, said that they
never heard a better song. There is a delicate hint that faced with
such a man, who had travelled so far, had met so many heroes, and
had received from these excellent people the greatest of praise, it
would be churlish to value the present song any less generously. And
then, having established himself by his impersonation as the equal of
this most successful of minstrels, the poet gracefully returns to the
present with an appropriate and persuasive generalization: all minstrels, like Widsith, go wandering through the world, and wherever
they go they meet one who is wise and open-handed, who desires to
gain fame before all perishes, light and life together.

4 The poet and his world

The role of the poet as one who called to mind the shared experience of the group[1] led him to emphasize the generic rather than the particular in his poems. Whatever the subject, whether people, landscape or the birds and animals which inhabit it, the stress is almost invariably on what is characteristic, predictable or habitual. The *Maxims* list and classify the categories of men to portray a world in which kings and queens distribute treasure, heroes ride out to battle and the thief passes by in the darkness. It is a static, emblematic world, where the noble is forever on horseback, accompanied by his *comitatus*, and the retainer remains at the foot of the gift-throne, his lord's hand on his head. Even the active pursuits of hawking, hunting, dicing, playing chess, sailing or playing the harp, are presented with the same lack of movement: men are fixed in their activities by the same inevitable processes that hold the dragon in its grave-mound, eternally guarding its treasure.

The same exemplary figures inhabit the universal world of the gnomic poetry and the more specific, individualized world of narrative and elegiac verse. The speaker in *The wanderer*, for instance, is an example of the exile who has learned wisdom through suffering. When he recalls the life of the hall from which he is now separated, the death of his lord and his present loneliness, he is expressing feelings which were common to all, in imagination even if not in reality. The status of the speaker as a representative of a class can be inferred from the interweaving of his account of his lord's burial and of his own wanderings with lines describing an unidentified, friendless exile, who may or may not be himself, and whose memory of the ceremonies of the hall contrasts so bitterly with the present reality of icy waves and sea-birds preening their feathers. The poet makes no attempt to distinguish the speaker from other exiles and lordless men: the exile who has buried his lord, the friendless man who observes nameless seabirds through the snow and hail, and the wise man who watches the dark winter storm beating on the rocky slopes as he broods on the decay of the society he has known, merge into a single figure, the platonic form, as it were, of exile.

[1] See p. 31 above.

Whereas the wanderer typifies that endurance which all should show in the face of inevitable adversity, the speaker of *The seafarer* carefully dissociates himself from the generality of men—symbolized by the man who lives comfortably on land—and this is right, because he calls men to a life of voluntary and exceptional hardship. In different ways, however, the two poems expand a single statement about the nature of the world, which might be expressed in the following gnomic form: 'It is characteristic of the wise man (and also his duty) to be alone in a wintry setting, to meditate on the passing of earthly splendour, and to draw consolation and resolution from his thoughts.' The characters exist as a means of expressing universal truths, not as individuals. Historical figures are presented in a similar way. The victory of Athelstan at Brunanburh is described in purely conventional terms. The slightly later account of the battle at Maldon appears at first sight to be more lifelike. The opening lines, with their impressionistic picture of the young man hawking by the river and the details of causeway and tides, suggest a desire for precision on the part of the poet. Byrhtnoth himself is portrayed in some detail: we see his careful disposition of his forces, his practical advice and encouragement, his superb irony as he addresses the messenger, his pleasure in fighting, his piety and the recklessness which he shares with figures like Hygelac. Once Byrhtnoth is dead, however, the narrative mode changes and the poem becomes a formulaic celebration of the principle that death by the side of one's lord is better than a shameful survival; the only exceptions to the procession of figures voicing identical sentiments of loyalty, gratitude, courage and family pride, are the sons of Odda who save themselves by flight. As in *The wanderer* and *The seafarer* the truth expressed by the poet is the truth of an ideal rather than the truth of individual lives.

The speeches of Byrhtnoth's *comitatus* serve as a reminder to fighting men, both within the poem and in the audience, of those principles which govern noble behaviour. In the same way, Cynewulf's warrior saints, Elene and Juliana, offer theological instruction to the audience; their speeches, though ostensibly addressed to characters within the poem, have virtually no dramatic or narrative function. The physical appearance of the characters, like their speech, is described only in relation to their role as saints. Of Elene we know only that she is *golde gehyrsted* (*Elene* 331), and of Juliana that she possesses a youthful radiance (*Juliana* 166–8 and 229). No further detail is needed: it is enough to know that Elene's appearance is that of a queen and that Juliana's virtue is outwardly apparent. Elsewhere women are described, as are Judith and Sarah, Abraham's wife, as *ælfsciene* 'elfin-bright'; some are pale-cheeked (*blachleor*) or curly-haired (*wundenlocc*); more frequently they are simply gold-adorned (*goldhroden*). Men in turn are characterized as *goldwlanc, goldhladen* or *goldbeorht.* Pictorial effect is unimportant: the gold ornaments of Wealhtheow and Ealhhild, the radiance of Judith and Juliana, the visored helmet of Beowulf are emblems, indicating to the audience the function of the characters in the poems. Wealth is a mark of esteem, beauty a sign of inner virtue and the wearing of arms an indication of valour. Wealhtheow, Freawaru, Hildeburh and Ealhhild are not differentiated from one another in any way; they are simply examples of womanliness, as it is described in the gnomic poetry:

Cyning sceal mid ceape   cwene gebicgan,
bunum ond beagum;   bu sceolon ærest
geofum god wesan.   Guð sceal in eorle,
wig geweaxan,   ond wif geþeon
leof mid hyre leodum,   leohtmod wesan,   85
rune healdan,   rumheort beon
mearum ond maþmum,   meodorædenne
for gesiðmægen   symle æghwær
eodor æþelinga   ærest gegretan,
forman fulle   to frean hond   90
ricene geræcan,   ond him ræd witan
boldagendum   bæm ætsomne.

Maxims I 81–92

A king should buy his queen for a price, with cups and rings; both must first be generous with presents. Warlike prowess should increase in a noble, and a woman should prosper, beloved among her people, be light of heart, keep secrets, be liberal with horses and treasures, always and everywhere before the group of companions greet the prince of nobles first with mead, quickly offer the first cups to the lord's hand, and know wisdom for both of the householders together.

Male characters tend to be classified in terms of opposing pairs: young and old, wise and foolish, generous and niggardly, brave and cowardly. Youth is associated with reckless daring and age with wisdom, qualities appropriate in turn to heroes and kings.[2] Heroes therefore are usually young, while kings are conventionally old and grey-haired. Categories can, however, be shifted. In the first part of *Beowulf* the two main characters, Beowulf and Hrothgar, are perfectly adapted to their roles: Beowulf is the brave young hero, Hrothgar the wise old king. Beowulf, despite his youth, possesses wisdom and is praised for it; Hrothgar, by contrast, realizes the limitations of his age

[2] R. E. Kaske, '*Sapientia et fortitudo* as the controlling theme of *Beowulf*', *SP* 55 (1958), pp. 423–56.

and does not attempt to go beyond them. As he says, the strength of his youth has passed. Hygelac, on the other hand, is a young king; he manifests the recklessness of youth but it is inappropriate to his other role, that of king, and it leads eventually to the downfall of his house. His son, Heardred, is likewise rash in his support of the exiled Swedish princes. Beowulf himself is portrayed in two roles: as the rash young hero in the first part of the poem and as the wise king in the second. Yet to some readers he has seemed to display heroic recklessness rather than kingly prudence when he fights the dragon. There is, of course, no choice for him and therefore no moral blame can attach to him—as Wiglaf says, 'He held on to his high destiny'—but there is always pathos in the spectacle of an old man being forced to fight, as can be seen from the description of the death of the aged Ongentheow at the hands of Wulf and Eofor (*Beowulf* 2961 ff). It is a pathos which arises at least partly from the expectation created by the gnomic poetry that a king's task is to sit in his hall, dispensing rings (*Maxims II* 28–9).

The predictive statements of the gnomic poetry suggest that there was an agreed view of nature and of landscape as well as of human behaviour. The world described in the Cotton gnomes is wet, windy and full of distant vistas. The skies are crossed by racing clouds; wind and thunder fill the air; grey water pours from the hills; clouds and water unite, flowing into the salt sea which surrounds all. Here and there green hills and blossoming groves are visible and, in the distance, the massive remains of ancient cities. Each creature has its appropriate place: the wolf and boar in the wood, the dragon in the cave, the bear on the heath, the salmon in the pool, the monster in the fen. Because the gnomic poetry is concerned with the essential nature of things, the landscape portrayed in it offers a stable and permanent backcloth for any kind of poetic statement. For example, the speaker in *The wanderer* describes a country filled with crumbling buildings, where the rocky slopes are battered by the storms of winter. The elements of the scene and the language in which they are expressed are commonplaces of Old English poetry; nothing is precise, for definition would be irrelevant in a poem whose theme is universal. Yet the landscape is more than an example of nature in harmony with man's thoughts. The inevitability which attaches to the wintry weather and the storm-swept ruins is transferred to the things which they symbolize, namely the decay of the civilized world.

In narrative poetry the gnomic idea that everything has its appointed place is extended to create a landscape which springs from the characters and their actions. The fenland of *Beowulf* (764, 820, 851, 1359) is necessary because it is the natural habitat for monsters such as Grendel and his mother (*Maxims II* 42–3); a grave-mound is required at the end of the poem, because it is characteristic of dragons to inhabit grave-mounds (*Maxims II* 26–7); the wood near the dragon's mound, like the wood in *The battle of Maldon*, offers a safe retreat for the cowardly. The more elaborate descriptions of the route to the monsters' lake, which seem at first to be less typical (*Beowulf* 1357–76, 1408–17), are equally dependent upon types and categories.[3] Hrothgar tells of an unknown land, wolf-infested slopes, windy headlands, a dangerous fen-path and a mountain-stream which disappears beneath the ground. The lake itself is overhung by frost-covered trees and its black waters leap up to mingle with the weeping skies. The foreboding effect produced by these passages comes from their universality of reference, from their expectedness rather than from anything new. The rocky slopes and headlands are standard features of the landscape in Old English poetry; mountain streams, according to the Cotton gnomes (*Maxims II* 47), are found in every land; fenland is the traditional home of monsters and demons (*Maxims II* 42–3); the wolf-slopes recall the association between wolves and outlaws (*Maxims I* 146–51) and the wolves which lurk on the edges of battle-fields. The account of the journey out to the lake (*Beowulf* 1408–17), with its emphasis on the narrowness and steepness of the paths, is equally predictable, for the defence of a narrow place is a typical heroic theme, and the mountain trees, water and grey rock of the lake itself evoke recognition, not surprise:

> Fyrgenbeamas
> ofer harne stan   hleonian funde,
> wynleasne wudu;   wæter under stod
> dreorig ond gedrefed.
>
> *Beowulf* 1414–17

He found mountain trees overhanging the grey rock, a joyless wood; the water lay beneath, bloodstained and murky.

The blood in the water recalls the previous journey to a lake, after the death of Grendel (*Beowulf* 847–52), but it is the grey rock which satisfies expectation. No other adjective is used in *Beowulf* to qualify the noun *stan*: the dragons of both Sigemund and Beowulf guard their hoards beneath identical grey rocks (*Beowulf* 887, 2553, 2744), and rightly so, for dragons are long-lived creatures and the adjective has connotations of age.

This propriety of landscape is not confined to sets for isolated

---

[3] For a different view of these passages see G. Storms, 'The subjectivity of the style of *Beowulf*', in *Studies in Old English literature in honor of Arthur G. Brodeur*, ed. S. B. Green-field, pp. 171–86, especially 184–85. See also M. Goldsmith, *The mode and meaning of Beowulf*, p. 114 on the symbolic treatment of the journey, and T. M. Andersson, *Early epic scenery*, pp. 145–59 for a possible connection with classical literature.

events or characters; it extends to the scenery of the poem as a whole. The same prospect of cliffs, headlands and sandy beaches characterizes Beowulf's arrival in Denmark, his return home and his fight against the dragon. The beaches are necessary for the launching and mooring of boats; headlands provide a lookout for coastguards or for the *comitatus* and, at the end, a fitting site for a funeral mound. But more than this, the agreement on a common scene, the lack of natural differences between the countries, helps unify the poem, giving visual expression to the idea of a heroic world in which ideals matter more than nationality.

This uniformity is one of the most striking things about the Old English poetic landscape. Homeric poetry, by contrast, is far more varied. The long roll-call of the Greek troops at the beginning of the *Iliad* (II 494–759), with its sequence of conventional epithets, distinguishes each region by some typical feature such as high hills, lawns or vineyards; the lands are steep, rocky, windy, wooded, flowery, deep in grass, with terraced hills, massive walls or white towers. The formulaic expressions for daybreak, a sea voyage or a journey by chariot are interspersed with descriptions of places so detailed that one feels one could walk through them. There is nothing in Old English poetry to compare with Telemachus's picture of Sparta with its clover, galingale, wheat, rye and barley, and the goat-pastures of Ithaca (*Odyssey IV* 602–608), or with the account of Calypso's island with its cave sheltered by alders, aspens and cypresses, its trailing vine and springs, and the meadows full of irises and parsley (*Odyssey V* 63–73), or with the description of Odysseus climbing the slope from the river mouth, concealing himself under the thorn and olive bushes and piling the dead leaves over himself (*Odyssey V* 475–87). In the whole of Old English poetry there is only one reference to a specific tree, the oak-tree in *The wife's lament*:

> Heht mec mon wunian   on wuda bearwe,
> under actreo   in þam eorðscræfe.
> Eald is þes eorðsele,   eal ic eom oflongad,
> sindon dena dimme,   duna uphea,   30
> bitre burgtunas,   brerum beweaxne,
> wic wynna leas.   Ful oft mec her wraþe begeat
> fromsiþ frean.   Frynd sind on eorþan,
> leofe lifgende,   leger weardiað,
> þonne ic on uhtan   ana gonge   35
> under actreo   geond þas eorðscrafu.
> Þær ic sittan mot   sumorlangne dæg,
> þær ic wepan mæg   mine wræcsiþas,
> earfoþa fela.

The wife's lament 27–39

They told me to live in the grove under an oak-tree in that earth-cave. This cave is old, I am all full of longing, the valleys are dark, the hills high, cheerless dwellings overgrown with briars, a joyless home. Often the departure of my lord came bitterly to mind. There are dear friends living on earth; they have a bed, while at dawn I go alone through this cave under the oak-tree. There I must sit the long summer's day, there I may weep for my exile, my many hardships.

Later in the poem (47–50) even this faint individuality disappears when the girl's lover is shown among the conventional storm-beaten rocky slopes. Even in the storm riddles (*Riddles 1–3*), which are among the most vivid descriptions of natural phenomena in Old English, there is no attempt to create a picture of any specific place.

Another distinctive feature of the Old English poetic landscape is its reliance on tone gradations rather than on differences in hue.[4] In part this results from the choice of subjects: storms and wintry weather are appropriately depicted in shades of black, white and grey. There are, however, places where a poet could have given the colour of something but has not done so. For example we are never told the colour of people's clothes, or the colours of the tapestries with which Heorot was hung (*Beowulf* 994–6), or the colour of the jewels on the cross in *The dream of the rood* (4–23). Instead we are made aware of light effects. The cross and the tapestries shine. The serpent in the garden of Eden (*Genesis* 899, 904, 913) is described as *fag*, a word which combines the meanings of shining, patterned and deceitful. The fleeing Israelites (*Exodus* 211–13) sit among the hills in shining clothes. Andrew, approaching the city of the Myrmedonians, sees buildings bright with variegated tiles (*Andreas* 842). Some poets distinguish between different kinds of light. The author of *The fight at Finnsburg*, for instance, sets the scene for the attack on the hall by contrasting the wavering moonlight with the light of fire or of sunrise:

> Ne ðis ne dagað eastan,   ne her draca ne fleogeð,
> ne her ðisse healle   hornas ne byrnað.
> Ac her forþ berað;   fugelas singað,   5
> gylleð græghama,   guðwudu hlynneð,
> scyld scefte oncwyð.   Nu scyneð þes mona
> waðol under wolcnum.
>
> *The fight at Finnsburg* 3–8

This is not the dawn from the east, nor does a dragon fly here, nor are the gables of this hall burning; but here men bear forth

4 Nigel F. Barley, 'Old English colour classification: where do matters stand?', *ASE* 3 (1974), pp. 15–28.

weapons, birds sing, the grey-coated one screams, the war-spear resounds, shield answers shaft. Now this wandering moon shines beneath the clouds.

The poet of *Beowulf* several times defines a scene in terms of its lighting. Grendel comes when the evening light is concealed under the bright sky (413–14), when, as night grows darker, shadowy forms move stealthily beneath the clouds (649–51). The fight in the underwater cave is lit by pale flames from the fire, quite different from the flood of sunshine which fills the cave once the monster has been killed (*Beowulf* 1570–72). The dragon's terrible attack is announced by the light from burning buildings:

Ða se gæst ongan	gledum spiwan,	
beorht hofu bærnan;	bryneleoma stod	
eldum on andan.	No ðær aht cwices	
lað lyftfloga	læfan wolde.	2315
Wæs þæs wyrmes wig	wide gesyne,	
nearofages nið	nean ond feorran,	
hu se guðsceaða	Geata leode	
hatode ond hynde;	hord eft gesceat,	
dryhtsele dyrnne,	ær dæges hwile.	2320
Hæfde landwara	lige befangen,	
bæle ond bronde,	beorges getruwode,	
wiges ond wealles;	him seo wen geleah.	

Beowulf 2312–23

Then the spirit began to spew out fire, to burn the bright buildings; the blaze of the fire shone out, terrifying men. Nor did the hostile flier in the air wish to leave anything alive there. The dragon's warring was seen far and wide, the fury of the hostile creature, from near and far, how the enemy attacked and injured the people of the Geats. He sped back again to his hoard, the splendid hidden cave, before daybreak. He had surrounded the people of the land with fire, with burning and flame, he trusted in his barrow, his warfare and the wall; his hope deceived him.

In addition to the many synonyms for light and dark some colour words seem to carry connotations of brightness or of surface texture.[5] The word *brun* is used of helmets and the edges of weapons, suggesting that the meaning is closer to modern 'gleaming' than to 'brown'; the word *fealo* 'yellow' may have a similar meaning when collocated with *stræte* (*Beowulf* 916). *Fealo* is most commonly used of water, however,

---

5 Barley, 'Colour classification', p. 24.

and it seems likely that the word involves an implied comparison with a ploughed field or perhaps with the brown of dead leaves.[6] The use of the word *fealo* illustrates the very stylized quality of Old English colour references. Stone, for instance, is almost invariably defined as grey, and this gives extra force to the description of the wall in *The ruin* (10) which is *ræghar ond readfah* 'red-coloured and grey with lichen'. Fire is frequently described as black, and the phrase *fyrswearta leg* (*Christ III* 983) suggests that this was the norm.[7] There are however one or two places where fire is described as *read* 'red', a word conventionally applied to gold and gold ornaments.[8] The choice made by a particular poet depends on symbolic criteria rather than naturalistic ones. The poet of *Christ III* uses only two colour words other than black and white. The blood-stained cross which comes to herald Christ's coming, and whose dazzling light drives off the shadows, is red (*Christ III* 1101); it replaces the sun, which has been blackened to the colour of blood:

> Þonne weorþeð sunne   sweart gewended
> on blodes hiw,   seo ðe beorhte scan
> ofer ærworuld   ælda bearnum.
>
> *Christ* 934–6

Then the sun, which used to shine brightly over the previous world for the sons of men, will be blackened to the colour of blood.

The cross is red not because of the blood but because it is the one object which breaks through the expanding darkness, of which the black fire forms a part.[9] In *Judgment day II*, on the other hand, it is the fire which is red, forming the one contrast to the blackness of sky, sun and moon (104–10, 147–58). The other colour word in *Christ III* is *grene*, which is used of the earth lamenting Christ's death, and which expresses a contrast between the living world and the death of its creator.

Grene is easily the most common Old English colour word after black and white, and is consistently used to symbolize life. It is a favourite word of the poet of *Genesis A*. Unlike the poet of *Genesis B*, who expresses the conflict between good and evil by means of a black and white world,[10] the poet of *Genesis A* contrasts what is black with

---

[6] *Maxims I* 52; *Andreas* 421, 1538, 1589; *Wanderer* 46; *Gifts of men* 53; *Battle of Brunanburh* 36; *Beowulf* 1950.
[7] *Genesis* 1926, 2417, 2543, 2858; *Christ III* 965, 966, 983, 994, 1532; *Judgment day I* 56.
[8] *Genesis* 2406; *Judith* 339; *Riddle 48* 6; *Soul and body II* 54; *Riddle 11* 2.
[9] *Christ III* 966, 983, 994, 1532.
[10] e.g. The two trees in paradise (*Genesis* 460–79). A more striking example is the trick by which the devil deceives Eve, making the earth and the heaven seem whiter (*hwitre* 603, 616).

what is green, so that goodness is seen in terms of fertility rather than radiance. Against the destructiveness of the black flood waters is set the green earth into which Noah and his family emerge from the ark (*Genesis* 1517); the black flames over Sodom swallow up all that is green (*Genesis* 2542–57); the chaos over which God broods after the fall of Satan is characterized by its lack of anything green and living:

> Folde wæs þa gyta
> græs ungrene;   garsecg þeahte
> sweart synnihte,   side and wide,
> wonne wægas.

Genesis 116–19

The earth, the grass was not yet green; far and wide, black and perpetual night covered the ocean, the dark waves.

The phrase *eorðe ælgrene* used of paradise (197), of the land given to Noah (1517) and of the land promised by God to Abraham (1787), symbolizes the living quality of God's creation. A rather similar phrase, *se grena wong*, describes the place which the defeated fiends are forced to relinquish in *Guthlac* (477, 746), and which becomes a paradise watched over by God. The paradise of the *Phoenix* (33–41) is a bower of green trees whose leaves never wither and whose fruits never fall.

This poem, which contains one of the few examples of overt allegory in Old English poetry, is equally remarkable for its colour symbolism. The phoenix was traditionally described as gaily-coloured. The passage in the Old English poem, which paints the bird in tones of green, brown and purple, with yellow feet, white-tipped wings and white-spotted tail (293–311), is closely based on part of the Lactantian *De ave phoenice*,[11] but this icon-like creation is set within a pattern of colour symbolism which seems original to the Old English poet. The phoenix lives in a paradise which is distinguished, as might be expected, by its greenness; the unwithered spring of the scene is expressed both through the choice of the word *grene* to describe the trees and grass and through the rejection of autumnal ideas implied in the line:

> Ne feallað þær on foldan   fealwe blostman.

Phoenix 74

Yet the bird itself is grey: *se haswa fugel* (121), for it is old:

[11] See *The phoenix*, ed. N. F. Blake, p. 91. The phoenix in the Old English prose version is equally bright: its feathers are gold like angels' wings, and its feet are red as blood, Blake, p. 95.

Ðonne bið gehefgad   haswigfeðra,
gomol, gearum frod,   grene eorðan
aflyhð, fugla wyn,   foldan geblowene,   155
ond þonne geseceð   side rice
middangeardes,   þær no men bugað
eard ond eþel.

Phoenix 153–8

Then the grey-feathered bird is weary, old, wise with years; the best of birds deserts the green place, the flowering earth, and seeks a broad kingdom in the world, a land and home where no men live.

The aged bird deserts the spring landscape for a waste place where it can build its nest and die; and here the poet takes up the contrast between spring and autumn which he had introduced in his original setting for the bird. The flames which consume the phoenix are not the traditional black ones; they are *fealo*: yellow, autumnal fires.

The decorative, contrived quality of the phoenix and of its home are an expression of a Christian aesthetic in which grace is contrasted with nature and goodness becomes synonymous with artifice.[12] But even in less openly Christian poetry there is the same preference for making natural phenomena serve a decorative end. One of the most obvious examples is the treatment of the theme of the beasts of battle. The variations on this theme, which range from the briefest possible mention of a single creature (*Elene* 52–3) to an explicit statement of the reason for their presence (*Judith* 205–12), allow the poets to imply the sameness of all battles and at the same time to give some specific emphasis. In *Elene* (110–13) it is the bloodthirsty enjoyment of the prospective feast, which prefigures the pleasure which Constantine's warriors derive from the battle; in *Exodus* (162–7) it is the indifference to suffering of the devouring beasts, which parallels the cold hostility of Pharaoh's army. Essentially, however, these passages are decorative additions to the paraphernalia of battle. In *The battle of Brunanburh* the focus is almost entirely on visual detail:

Letan him behindan   hræw bryttian   60
saluwigpadan,   þone sweartan hræfn,
hyrnednebban,   and þane hasewanpadan,
earn æftan hwit,   æses brucan,
grædigne guðhafoc   and þæt græge deor,
wulf on wealde.   65

Battle of Brunanburh 60–65

---

[12] Daniel G. Calder, 'The vision of paradise: a symbolic reading of "The phoenix"', *ASE* 1 (1972), pp. 167–81.

They left behind them the dark-coated black raven, horny-beaked, and the grey-coated eagle with white tail, to enjoy the dead, make use of the carrion, the greedy warhawk and that grey beast, the wolf in the wood.

Elsewhere it is the emotional content which matters. Because the beasts are regularly associated with battle they can evoke feelings connected with fighting when they appear elsewhere. In *The wanderer* (81–3) a brief reference to bird and wolf in the passage on the decay of the world is enough to call to mind the ravages of war and the various forms of death. In *Beowulf* the prophetic speech by the messenger indicates his expectation of the two great misfortunes of the heroic world, exile and war:

> Forðon sceall gar wesan
> monig, morgenceald,   mundum bewunden,
> hæfen on handa,   nalles hearpan sweg
> wigend weccean,   ac se wonna hrefn
> fus ofer fægum   fela reordian,   3025
> earne secgan   hu him æt æte speow,
> þenden he wið wulf   wæl reafode.
>
> *Beowulf* 3021–7

Therefore many a spear, cold in the morning, shall be raised up, grasped in the hands; the music of the harp shall not wake the warriors, but the black raven shall fly swiftly over the doomed men, relate many things, tell the eagle how he fared at the feasting while he competed with the wolf to rob the dead.

Here it is not the disposal of the corpses and the subsequent feeling of loss which matters, as in *The wanderer*, but the shrinking from foreseen miseries, the chill of early morning, the lack of civilized entertainment and the constant reminders of death. But although the raven is part of the furniture of war it is not in itself symbolic of war. When separated from its friends the eagle and the wolf it can be a joyful creature, almost domesticated:

> Gæst inne swæf
> oþþæt hrefn blaca   heofones wynne
> bliðheort bodode.
>
> *Beowulf* 1800–02

The guest slept within until the black raven cheerfully announced the joy of heaven.

Another bird which operates in two quite different emotional areas is the cuckoo, associated in later periods with spring merry-making, but in Old English with sorrow, especially the sorrow of a journey. The best-known example is in *The seafarer* where the cuckoo is one of the harbingers of spring which urge the traveller to set out on the sea:

> Swylce geac monað   geomran reorde,
> singeð sumeres weard,   sorge beodeð
> bitter in breosthord.
>
> *Seafarer* 53–5

Similarly the cuckoo admonishes him with its sad voice; the guardian of summer sings, announces bitter sorrow to the heart.

In the same way the speaker of *The husband's message* urges the listener to set out on the sea, travelling south, when the cuckoo is heard:

>   Heht nu sylfa þe
> lustum læran,   þæt þu lagu drefde,
> siþþan þu gehyrde   on hliþes oran
> galan geomorne   geac on bearwe.
>
> *Husband's message* 20–23

Now he commands me to tell you joyfully that you should set out on the sea after you have heard the sad cuckoo crying in the grove on the edge of the hill.

The cuckoo, like the raven, illustrates the lack of a standard set of associations for these birds, for in *Guthlac* it is part of a pleasant spring scene, the earthly paradise to which Guthlac returns after overcoming the devils:

> Smolt wæs se sigewong   ond sele niwe,
> fæger fugla reord,   folde geblowen;
> geacas gear budon.
>
> *Guthlac* 742–4

Gentle was the plain of victory and new the dwelling, fair the voice of the birds, the land blossoming; cuckoos announced the time of year.

Just as the raven is part of the scenery of battle so the cuckoo is part of the picture of spring, and spring can be associated either with the temperate pleasant weather of the earthly paradise or with the season when one sets out on the sea and which is therefore sad because of departure. Interestingly, in *The husband's message* the voyage—whether of a wife joining her husband or the human soul following Christ—should be a happy one, and the sad voice of the cuckoo must be conventional.

Yet there are times when poets give up this patterned approach to the natural world in favour of something less predictable. Here and there in *Beowulf* are pictures which are very sharply defined, not through a full and detailed description—a technique reserved for pictures of weapons and armour—but through a single well-chosen phrase, which allows one suddenly to visualize the scene. For example, in the rather stylized account of the swimming match against Breca Beowulf says of the monsters:

> Ac on mergenne   mecum wunde
> be yðlafe   uppe lægon,
> sweordum aswefede.
>
> *Beowulf* 565–7

But in the morning, wounded by swords, they lay up among the leavings of the waves, put to sleep by the swords.

The word *yðlaf* refers to the debris of wood and seaweed left by the waves as the tide goes down. Through his choice of this word the poet has created a vivid picture of a line of monsters stranded high on the beach together with the other odds and ends thrown up by the tide. When the warriors set out in pursuit of Grendel's mother they see her tracks *æfter waldswaþum* (1403). The word *swaþu* is related to the modern word 'swathe' and the compound *wald-swaþu* implies that the monster had trampled down a swathe of trees in her passage through the forest just as people trample the grass or corn in their passage through a field.[13] Finally, in the description of the funeral pyre (3143–8) the poet adds one significant detail to the account of the black smoke rising from the fire: the wind had died down. With this one phrase he evokes a picture of the column of smoke rising straight up to the sky.[14]

Another way in which the *Beowulf* poet allows his audience to visualize things is by focusing attention on different kinds of movement. The dragon, for instance, coils itself together before attacking Beowulf:

> Ða se wyrm gebeah
> snude tosomne;   he on searwum bad.

[13] Storms, 'Style of *Beowulf*', p. 184.
[14] M. Daunt, 'Minor realism and contrast in *Beowulf*', in *Mélanges de linguistique et de philologie: Fernand Mossé in memoriam*, pp. 87–94, especially p. 91.

Gewat ða byrnende   gebogen scriðan,
to gescipe scyndan.

Beowulf 2567–70

Then the worm coiled itself quickly together; he waited in his
armour. Then it moved forward, burning and sinuous, hurrying
to its fate.

But perhaps his preferred way of bringing a scene to life is not pictorial at all but based on sounds. The mailcoats of Beowulf's men rattle
as they disembark (226–7); the ring-mail echoes as they march (322–
3); the wooden floor of Heorot resounds as men tramp across it
(1317); its structure groans during the fight with Grendel (767–70);
there is the cheerful sound of conversation (611, 1160–61); weapons
sing songs as they strike the enemy (1521–22); ships creak as they
drive through the waves (1906); Beowulf's voice echoes beneath the
dragon's rock, and the earth itself resounds during the fight (2558).
Other poets are equally sensitive to sound distinctions. The poet of
Andreas had clearly experienced the sounds made by a sailing boat in
heavy seas, in particular the grinding noise as the waves hit the boat
and the clatter of rigging and sails:

Wedercandel swearc,
windas weoxon,   wægas grundon,
streamas styredon,   strengas gurron,
wædo gewætte.

Andreas 372–5

The candle of the sky darkened, the winds increased, the waves
ground against the boat, the currents were stirred up, the rigging
rattled, the wet sails.

The magnificent description of the end of the world in *Christ III*
includes many splendid visual images, among them the smoky flame
advancing like an angry warrior (983–4), the stars scattered from the
sky (939–40) and tossed about by the storm, cliffs melting into the sea
(977–81) or the water burning like wax (988). Yet the chief effect of
the passage comes from the sound; the constant roaring and crashing,
the piercing notes of the angels' trumpets (878–85), the echoing
depths of creation, the roaring of the flame (930, 932) the howling of
the winds (949–50) and the weeping of mankind (997–9).

    Finally, poets liked to define objects according to their method of
construction. Many of the traditional phrases in Old English poetry
contain references to technical details: coats of mail are *heard hondlocen*
(*Beowulf* 322, 551), ships are either bound or nailed together,[15] swords

---

[15] *Beowulf* 216, 1910; *Riddle 58* 5; *Genesis* 1418, 1433.

have twisted blades—a reference to the technique of pattern-welding—or are described as left by the files or hammers,[16] buildings are fastened together by iron clamps.[17] Some of the riddles offer detailed descriptions of the making of books or the form of ploughs or rakes, and the poet of *The ruin* notes the structural niceties of the Roman remains with the same care that he devotes to their emotional appeal.

From all this two features emerge which characterize the abstraction made by the Old English poet from the world around him: a liking for pattern and a love of artifice.

The patterned, ordered element shows itself in three inter-related ways. The world is seen as something which is controlled, and this control takes the form of a conflict and at the same time a sequence. God sits above all, unchanging and directing all; beneath him is man whose essence is change:

> Meotud sceal in wuldre,   mon sceal on eorþan
> geong ealdian.   God us ece biþ,
> ne wendað hine wyrda   ne hine wiht dreceþ,
> adl ne yldo   ælmihtigne;   10
> ne gomelað he in gæste,   ac he is gen swa he wæs,
> þeoden geþyldig.

Maxims I 7–12

God must live in glory, man on earth must pass from youth to age. God is everlasting in comparison with us, events do not change him nor does anything, whether sickness or age, afflict the almighty; he does not grow old in spirit, but is always as he was, a patient lord.

It is not only man who grows old: the whole of nature is equally subject to the effects of time:

> Yldo beoð on eorðan   æghwæs cræftig;
> mid hiðendre   hildewræsne,
> rumre racenteage,   ræceð wide,
> langre linan,   lisseð eall ðæt heo wile.   295
> Beam heo abreoteð   and bebriceð telgum,
> astyreð standendne   stefn on siðe,
> afilleð hine on foldan;   friteð æfter ðam
> wildne fugol.   Heo oferwigeð wulf,

---

[16] *Beowulf* 1521, 1616, 1032 *fela laf*; 2829 *homera laf*. It is possible that the word *brun-ecg* is another reference to technique, for the brown colour of the metal was crucial in judging the correct temperature in the tempering process, see W. Waddilove, 'Basic blacksmithing', *Practical self-sufficiency* 6 (Oct.–Nov. 1976), pp. 26–28, p. 28. I am indebted to Mr. C. Stedman for this reference.

[17] *Beowulf* 774, 998.

hio oferbideð stanas,   heo oferstigeð style,   300
hio abiteð iren mid ome,   deð usic swa.

Solomon and Saturn 292–301

On earth age has power over all; it reaches far and wide with its
capturing battle-chain, its extended fetter, its long rope, and binds
all that it wishes. It destroys the tree and breaks the twigs, uproots
the standing trunk on its journey and fells it to the ground; after
that it devours the wild bird. It overpowers the wolf, outlasts the
rocks, surpasses steel, bites iron with rust, and treats us likewise.

This destructive power, summed up in the word *wyrd* 'the course of
events', is analogous to Boethius's 'fate' it is subject to God and therefore an example of order.[18] This idea is expressed very clearly in the
following passage where Christ's glory, the power of events and the
cycle of the seasons are closely linked:

              Þrymmas syndan Cristes myccle,
wyrd byð swiðost.   Winter byð cealdost,   5
lencten hrimigost   (he byð lengest ceald),
sumor sunwlitegost   (swegel byð hatost),
hærfest hreðeadegost,   hæleðum bringeð
geres wæstmas,   þa þe him god sendeð.

Maxims II 4–9

The powers of Christ are great; the course of events is strongest.
Winter is coldest, spring most frosty (it remains cold longest),
summer is most sunny (the sky is warmest), autumn is most triumphant, it brings to men the fruits of the year which God sends
them.

The idea that the seasons are under God's direct control is not
confined to the gnomic poetry. In *Beowulf* (1607–11), as in *Maxims I*
(74–7), God is shown unbinding the fetters of winter, and in *Christ and
Satan* (11–12) he numbers the drops of rain. Not only does God's
creation decay: it is founded on strife:

God sceal wið yfele,   geogoð sceal wið yldo,   50
lif sceal wið deaþe,   leoht sceal wið þystrum,
fyrd wið fyrde,   feond wið oðrum,
lað wið laþe   ymb land sacan,
synne stælan.   A sceal snotor hycgean
ymb þysse worulde gewinn.   55

Maxims II 50–55

[18] cf *Wanderer* 85; *Seafarer* 103.

Good shall oppose evil, youth shall be in conflict with age, life will fight death, light against darkness, army against army, enemy against other, foe against foe contend throughout the land, impute evil. The wise man must always meditate on the strife in this world.[19]

The picture is familiar from *Beowulf* where not only is the story based on conflict between good and evil—the light of Heorot against the darkness of Grendel—but landscape and weather are composed of conflicting elements: the dark lake with its frost-hung trees is an area of perpetual winter in what is otherwise a sunny springlike scene. In *Beowulf* nature appears as a symbol of the underlying feuds in the world. Elsewhere it is an expression of God's power. In describing the world around them Old English poets constantly focused on the craftsmanship of men's creations; in the same way they depicted the natural order as God's work of art. The poet of *Christ I* portrays God as an architect who will rebuild the ruined house of mankind:

> Gesweotula nu þurh searocræft   þin sylfes weorc,
> soðfæst, sigorbeorht,   ond sona forlæt   10
> weall wið wealle.   Nu is þam weorce þearf
> þæt se cræftga cume   ond se cyning sylfa,
> ond þonne gebete,   nu gebrosnad is,
> hus under hrofe.
>
> *Christ* 9–14

Make plain now your own work through your skill, true and victorious one, and at once leave standing wall against wall. Now it is necessary for the work that the craftsman should come and the king himself and make good what is now ruined, the house beneath its roof.

The comparison of the human body to a house is a commonplace of Old English poetry, and words such as *sawelhus*, *gasthof*, *licfæt* or *bancofa* are so frequent that the metaphor tends to disappear. Occasionally however the words recover their original implications, as in Cynewulf's descriptions of the fortress of the soul with its wall, gate and tower, and of man's body as a house which must be built on a foundation of living stone in order to withstand the storms of sin (*Juliana* 397–403, 647–54).
God's craftsmanship is shown more often as that of a goldsmith.

---

[19] cf Ecclesiasticus xxxiii 13–15, T. D. Hill, 'Notes on the Old English "Maxims" I and II', *N & Q* 215 (1970), pp. 445–7. A contrasting view is given by the poet of *The order of the world* (82–5) who portrays God reconciling opposing forces to create order.

The verb *frætwian* and the related noun *frætwe* are commonly used of created things. The best example is, of course, *The phoenix*.[20] The *Beowulf* poet describes God decorating the earth with leaves and branches (96–7), the *Menologion* (207) talks of the green plains as the ornaments of the earth and the sun, moon and stars are frequently described as jewels in the sky.[21] Just as those things which shine in heaven are seen as jewels because of their brightness, so too the eyes are considered as jewels set in man's head. The two metaphors are linked in the following passage on a blind man, where the misery of blindness is defined as a lack of congruity between man and his environment: the jewels of the eyes cannot gaze on the jewels of the heavens:

> Blind sceal his eagna þolian,
> oftigen biþ him torhtre gesihþe. Ne magon hi tunglu be-
> witian, 40
> swegltorht sunnan ne monan; þæt him biþ sar in his mode,
> onge þonne he hit ana wat, ne weneð þæt him þæs
> edhwyrft cyme.
> Waldend him þæt wite teode, se him mæg wyrpe syllan,
> hælo of heofodgimme, gif he wat heortan clæne.
>
> *Maxims I* 39–44

The blind man must endure the loss of his eyes, bright sight is taken from him. Nor can they gaze on the stars, the bright sun and moon; that causes him sorrow in heart, when he alone knows it, nor does he expect that a change will come to him. God gave him that torment, he can give him a cure, health for the jewels of the head, if he knows his heart is clean.

Immaterial things are seen in the same symbolic context: man's thoughts and words are described in terms borrowed from the treasure-hoard, for speech was to be stored and treasured, and even the emotions are hammered and wrought in the forge by the misery-smiths and laughter-smiths.[22]

This view of the world coincides with the Old English view of poetry. Artistry is the supreme form of control. God is the great craftsman who creates a world which testifies to his art. Man is not only an example of God's artistry: he is himself an artist, creating well-made weapons and beautiful jewels. His art does not imitate nature; instead, nature is seen as imitating art; there is no admiration

[20] See p. 55 above.
[21] *Guthlac* 1212; *Christ* 692; *Genesis* 956, 2191.
[22] *teonsmiþas, Guthlac* 205; *hleahtorsmiþas, Exodus* 43.

here for a world untouched by man. Poetry, like jewellery, is the product of skill not inspiration.[23] In exercising his art the poet imitates and shares in God's creation, and it is to be expected, therefore, that his work will share the order and elaboration which typify God's work.

[23] See Chapter 2 above.

*Poetic
art and form*

⑤ Poetic form

The conditions under which Old English poetry was composed and the attitude of the Anglo-Saxons to their poets governed to a large extent the form their poetry took. The conception of the poet as the inheritor of a tradition—whether it was the oral tradition of the group or the bookish tradition of the scholar—together with the emphasis on art as craftsmanship rather than inspiration, was conducive to the development of forms which were innovatory only within very narrow limits. Content was familiar—even commonplace—and presentation was conventional. Furthermore, poetic authority seems to have required that the poet should draw attention to his borrowings rather than that he should integrate them by expressing them anew. The use of a traditional vocabulary and of set-piece descriptions is common throughout Old English poetry, as it is in much early literature outside Old English, but many Old English poets go beyond this simple traditionalism to create poems whose essence is quotation.[1]

One of the more obvious examples of quotation is the poem *Widsith*, which consists of three lists of kings, tribes or heroes, each with a distinctive syntax and rhythm, interspersed with passages about Widsith himself. The poem is devised to glorify its fictive speaker and, through him, its actual speaker, and this is achieved partly through an assumed identification of the two and partly by allowing both to speak in words taken from the poetry of the past. The poet implies that he himself is of the same kind as the fictive Widsith, contemporary of Eormanric (d. 375), and Widsith in turn, through his recitation of the three lists with their archaic rhythms, identifies himself with an even more distant past, to affirm the unity and timelessness of the poet's art. The quotation is essential to the poet's purpose and must therefore be made obvious to his audience.

Two other poems which depend for part of their effect on recognizable quotation are *The wanderer* and *The seafarer*. The speaker of *The wanderer* encloses his own thoughts (58–87) between those of two

[1] The word 'quotation' is used here of borrowings from a group of works or from a tradition which stand out from the surrounding passages even though they do not necessarily use the exact words of one specific work. The technique is similar to that of parts of Eliot's *The waste land* and *Four quartets*.

fictive characters: the exile who remembers his dead lord (6–57) and the wise man who reflects on the transitory pleasures which have been overturned by time (88–110). The essential feature of these two characters is their generality, something which encroaches even on the central part of the poem in the figures of the wise man who is moderate in all things and the man who sees in the ruins of the past an image of what is to come. If these characters are to be truly representative then they must speak and think within a tradition which is familiar to all, for what is novel cannot inspire universal assent. The expression of traditional material in traditional language, which might seem shallow were the poet speaking in his own person, supplies the continuity with the past which the theme of the poem requires. Continuity is important because the poem involves a passage on the part of the speaker from regret for the past to hope in the future and at the same time an ability to grasp that the ruins of the past provide both an image of future destruction and, paradoxically, an assurance of security against destruction, the *fæstnung* of the final line. The two most obviously conventional passages—the lines on death (78–84) and the lament for the passing of heroic society (92–110)—form part of this prophetic image which unites past with future:

> Ongietan sceal gleaw hæle   hu gæstlic bið,
> þonne ealre þisse worulde wela   weste stondeð,
> swa nu missenlice   geond þisne middangeard   75
> winde biwaune   weallas stondaþ,
> hrime bihrorene,   hryðge þa ederas.
> Woriað þa winsalo,   waldend licgað
> dreame bidrorene,   duguþ eal gecrong,
> wlonc bi wealle.   Sume wig fornom,   80
> ferede in forðwege,   sumne fugel oþbær
> ofer heanne holm,   sumne se hara wulf
> deaðe gedælde,   sumne dreorighleor
> in eorðscræfe   eorl gehydde.
>
> *Wanderer* 73–84

The wise man must understand how terrifying it will be when the wealth of all this earth stands waste, as now here and there throughout this world walls stand, blown on by the wind, hung with frost, the buildings swept by snow. The wine-halls crumble, the rulers lie dead, deprived of joy, all the tried warriors have fallen, proud by the rampart. Some war carried off, bore on their death-journey, one a bird carried over the high sea, one the grey wolf divided in death, one a sad-faced earl hid in a grave.

The syntax of this passage, with its repeated *sumne*, recalls that of poems like *The gifts of men* and *The fortunes of men* discussed below, but the content, with its distribution of the ways of disposing of the body, is related to the mnemonics and classificatory systems of works like Byrhtferth's *Manual* or, less respectably, the prose *Solomon and Saturn*.[2] The form of the reference marks the quotation as a learned rather than a heroic one. Whereas the *eardstapa* of the beginning of the poem thinks of death in the context of loss of friends, kinsmen and lord, the *gleaw hæle* of line 73 sees it as something to be analysed, and it is this analysis which allows the poet to make the transition from regret to acceptance. Similarly, the lament for the heroic world (92–6) combines the vocabulary of heroic verse with a form taken from homiletic writings.[3] By his choice of form and, in particular, by his use of the phrase *swa heo no wære*, the poet places his wise man firmly within the Christian tradition, relating him to figures like Boethius's Wisdom who says:

Hwær synt nu þæs Welondes ban, oððe hwa wat nu hwær hi wæron? Oððe hwær is nu se foremæra and se aræda Romwara heretoga, se wæs haten Brutus, oðre naman Cassius? Oððe se wisa and fastræda Cato, se wæs eac Romana heretoga; se wæs openlice uðwita. Hu ne wæran þas gefyrn forðgewitene? and nan mon nat hwær hi nu sint. Hwæt is heora nu to lafe, butan se lytla hlisa and se nama mid feaum stafum awriten?[4]

The set-piece description of darkness, storm and rocky slopes which follows is not heroic either: the solitary survivor of *Beowulf* 2231–70 makes no mention of wintry weather, nor does the father mourning for his son (*Beowulf* 2444–62), and the exile of the messenger's prophetic speech is associated only with the chill of battle (*Beowulf* 3015–27). The only real parallel is the *Seafarer* 31–3 though the poet of *The order of the world* has a description of the day coming up over the misty slopes and of the snow falling as day dawns in the east (59–63); in the second case, at least, the weather has religious connotations. A possible clue to the overtones of the passage in *The wanderer* comes in the

---

[2] *Byrhtferth's Manual*, ed. S. J. Crawford, EETS 177 (1929), pp. 198–227 and *The dialogue of Salomon and Saturnus*, ed. J. M. Kemble, pp. 178–93. References to the different ways of disposing of the body are found in various Greek and Latin texts and in two Old English homilies, though the inclusion of the wolf is confined to *The wanderer* and *The fortunes of men*, see J. E. Cross, 'On *The wanderer* lines 80–84', *Vetenskaps-Societens í Lund Årsbok* (1958–9), pp. 77–110. An eagle and a wolf are shown dismembering the bodies in the drawing of the massacre of the innocents in the Bury St Edmunds Psalter, Vatican Regin. lat. 12, f. 87ᵛ.

[3] J. E. Cross, ' "Ubi sunt" passages in Old English', *Vetenskaps-Societetens í Lund Årsbok* (1956), pp. 25–44.

[4] *Boethius*, ed. Sedgefield, p. 46, XIX = Latin ii, met. 7.

verse *Solomon and Saturn* (292–326). The second dialogue contains a
series of passages on decay: the destructive power of old age, the
crushing weight of snow, the withering of leaves and the sea flowing
over the land at doomsday. In the middle are the following two lines:

> Nieht bið wedera ðiestrost,   ned bið wyrda heardost,
> sorg bið swarost byrðen,   slæp bið deaðe gelicost.

Solomon and Saturn 312–13

Night is the darkest of weathers, need is the hardest of fates,
sorrow is the heaviest burden, sleep is most like death.

There are none of the verbal correspondences of *The wanderer* and *The
seafarer*, which imply the existence of a theme with a set form, but the
ideas are similar, and this suggests that the lines in *The wanderer* like
the earlier reference to the ways of death are meant to recall something from wisdom literature. A point of especial interest is the linking
in *Solomon and Saturn*, as in *The wanderer* and *The seafarer*, of wintry
weather and judgment. If this does represent a traditional association
of ideas then the miserable weather of *The wanderer* (101–5), like the
crumbling walls, is an image of the approaching end rather than a
simple reflection of human mood.
In *The wanderer* quotation is used to characterize the speaker as a
reincarnation of the wise men of the past. In *The seafarer* the same
themes recur, sometimes in almost the same words, but their context,
and therefore their emphasis, is different.
The seafarer, unlike *The wanderer*, claims autobiographical status: the
poet does not derive his authority from a hypothetical wise man, and
his conclusion lacks the impersonality of the wanderer's; for him
heaven is the home which he will share with his listeners. The snow-
storm of lines 31–3 is something from the past: it has brought him to
his present state but, in contrast to the similar passage in *The wanderer*,
it has no relevance to his future. The lines on the passing of earthly
glory, which are superficially similar to the wanderer's lament, are in
reality quite different in regard both to content and to frame. There
are no visible remains of the past: the repeated *dagas sind gewitene* and
dreamas sind gewitene, and the allusion to the pitiful successors of the
kings and emperors, draw attention to the physical and moral emptiness of the scene. The old man of lines 91–6 typifies the world which
is already dying. This poet needs no figure of authority to prophesy
from the ruins of the past, because he knows already that this world
cannot last. His audience, too, must have known, for there is an
assumption on the poet's part of familiarity not only with the themes
of homiletic writing but with their vocabulary: the world stirs into
new life and at the same time hastens to its end (*onetteð* 49); man is a

stranger in this world *(elpeodigra* 38); his hope lies elsewhere *(hyht* 45).

In *The seafarer* one sees the part played by the audience in the creation of poetic forms: the poet controls and develops the argument but leaves his listeners to grasp its implications for themselves. Other poets went further in this direction, creating works whose form was implicit rather than stated. Among the Old English poems which have been preserved, about eight or nine consist of lists. In some the shape has been imposed from without: *The rune poem* follows the order of the *fuþorc*; the shape of *The fates of the apostles* depends on the number of the apostles; the ten divisions of *Precepts* may be intended to remind one of the decalogue. Other poems, such as the Cotton and Exeter *Maxims* or the poems on the gifts and fates of men, seem at first sight to be purely random collections. Closer study shows, however, that they have a logical form but it is one which has to be created by the audience within limits defined by the poet.

Two of these poems, *The gifts of men* and *The fortunes of men*, draw together various activities, skills and misfortunes and frame them with opening and closing paragraphs which direct the thoughts of the reader. The lists themselves were probably stereotyped collections, for something similar appears in Cynewulf's ascension poem, *Christ II* (664–85).[5] This last passage is derived, at least indirectly, from part of the Epistle to the Ephesians (iv 7–12) which describes the ascending Christ as a king bestowing gifts on his followers, but Cynewulf substitutes for St Paul's gifts ones more appropriate to an Anglo-Saxon audience: poetry, music, knowledge of law and star-craft, fighting, seamanship, tree-climbing and the making of weapons. Not only are the lists similar in *Christ* and in *The gifts of men*; their implications are similar, for both poets remark that God shares his gifts widely, so that no man can become too proud of his many skills.[6] The two passages are not sufficiently close, however, to imply quotation from some pre-existing source; rather they suggest the re-expression of a well-known theme. It is this common element which allows the audience to participate in the making of the poem.

The gifts of men and *The fortunes of men*, like the *Maxims*, *Precepts* and *Solomon and Saturn*, belong to a well-established kind of writing, that of wisdom literature. The genre is almost universal and the proverbial material at least must have been very well known. There is also a biblical component, and this too is of a quite obvious kind. The theme of *The gifts of men* is related to two biblical images: the Pauline idea of the body of Christ all of whose members are equal (Rom. xii 3–8), and Christ's parable about the talents and the proper use of God's

---

[5] J. E. Cross, 'The Old English poetic theme of "the gifts of men" ', *Neophilologus* 46 (1962), pp. 66–70.
[6] One half-line is identical in the two poems: *Christ* 684b and *Gifts of men* 100b.

gifts (Matt. xxv 14–30).[7] It differs from these biblical passages however in being neither didactic nor homiletic. In form, the poem is a hymn, praising God's generosity and discretion. Like the psalms which are classified as hymns (e.g. Psalm viii), it consists of three parts: a statement about God's kindness to man, a list of motives for praising God, and a repetition of the opening statement together with an invitation to prayer. But although the structure is similar, the content of the central part is quite different, for the psalms tend to stress God's works of creation or of deliverance while the Old English poet, like the author of Ecclesiasticus, emphasizes human skills, seeing them as examples of God's beneficence:

> Next let us praise illustrious men,
>   our ancestors in their successive generations.
> The Lord has created an abundance of glory,
>   and displayed his greatness from earliest times.
> Some wielded authority as kings
>   and were renowned for their strength;
> others were intelligent advisers
>   and uttered prophetic oracles.
> Others directed the people by their advice,
>   by their understanding of the popular mind,
>   and by the wise words of their teaching;
> others composed musical melodies,
>   and set down ballads;
> others were rich and powerful,
>   living peacefully in their homes.
> All these were honoured by their contemporaries,
>   and were the glory of their day.
> Some of them left a name behind them,
>   so that their praises are still sung.
> While others have left no memory,
>   and disappeared as though they had not existed,
> they are now as though they had never been,
>   and so too, their children after them.
>
>   Ecclesiasticus xliv 1–9

Again there is a difference, for while the Old English poet retains the biblical idea that men's numerous activities are examples of divine order and fecundity, he does not go on, as does the author of Ecclesiasticus, to meditate on the ephemeral nature of these activities. He is content simply to give thanks.

[7] Cross, 'Gifts of men', *Neophilologus* 46, pp. 66–70; D. D. Short, '*Leoðocræftas* and the Pauline analogy of the body in the Old English *Gifts of men*', *Neophilologus* 59 (1975), pp. 463–5.

This central section of the poem, though skilfully arranged and varied in presentation, is illustrative rather than sequential: in places there is a contrast, as between the man brave in battle and the one wise in council (39–43), or a similarity, as between the jeweller and the weaponsmith (58–66), but there is no steady progression towards some end. The only form imposed by the poet derives from the opening and closing lines.

The main theme of the poem is the judgment of God, who ensures that no one should be deprived of all gifts lest he should despair, and that no one should receive all gifts lest he should grow too proud. The contrast between the two points is neatly expressed through a syntax which draws attention to the comparison without becoming repetitive:

I   *Ne bi∂ ænig þæs*   earfo∂sælig
    mon on moldan,   ne þæs medspedig,
    lytelhydig,   ne þæs læthydig,   10
    þæt hine se argifa   ealles biscyrge
    modes cræfta   oþþe mægendæda,
    wis on gewitte   oþþe on wordcwidum,
    þy læs ormod sy   ealra þinga,
    þara þe he geworhte   in woruldlife,   15
    geofona gehwylcre.   *Næfre god deme∂*
    þæt ænig eft   *þæs earm geweor∂e.*
II *Nænig eft þæs swiþe*   þurh snyttrucræft
    in þeode þrym   þisses lifes
    for∂ gestige∂,   *þæt him* folca weard   20
    þurh his halige giefe   hider onsende
    wise geþohtas   ond woruldcræftas,
    under anes meaht   ealle forlæte,
    þy læs he for wlence   wuldorgeofona ful,
    mon mode swi∂   of gemete hweorfe   25
    ond þonne forhycge   heanspedigran.

                                Gifts of men 8–26

There is no man on earth so unblessed or so poorly endowed, so small-minded or so dull of thought, that the generous Lord will deprive him of all skill of mind or great deeds, wise in mind or in speech, in case he despairs of everything which he did in this world, every gift. God would never decree that any man should become so wretched. Again, no man will prosper so much through his wisdom, through his glory among the people in this life, that the guardian of nations through his holy gift will send here to him wise thoughts and worldly skills, let all these come into the power of one man, in case he in his pride, full of glorious gifts, a man great in mind, turns from moderation and then despises the less fortunate man.

The general shape of the two sections is similar: *Ne bið ænig* . . . *þæt hine* . . . *þy læs* in the first section; *Nænig* . . . *þæt him* . . . *þy læs* in the second. Within this broad framework the ideas are expressed quite differently: in the first section the poet piles up adjectives, *earfoðsælig, medspedig, lytelhydig, læthydig,* drawing attention to the list by the assonance of the endings and the repetition of the word *þæs*; in the second section he picks up the words with which the first statement ends, *ænig eft þæs earm geweorðe,* and modifies them to *nænig eft þæs swiþe* . . . *forð gestigeð* to emphasize the contrast. The two sections are linked by logic as well as by syntax, for the less fortunate man who may be despised by the successful man of the second statement is the same as the despairing man of the first statement. And whereas the first statement, about the poor man, ends with an emphatic reiteration that God would never allow such utter destitution, the second passage ends with a reiteration, not of the fact that God does not allow pride, but of a point which relates back to the whole passage:

> Ac he gedæleð,   se þe ah domes geweald,
> missenlice   geond þisne middangeard
> leoda leoþocræftas   londbuendum.
>
> *Gifts of men* 27–9

But he who has power to judge distributes the bodily skills of men variously to those living in this world.

The noun *domes* (27) echoes the verb *demað* at the end of the first statement (16). The immediate reference in both passages is to God's power of discrimination in this world, but both words inevitably hint at God's final judgment, so that human abilities are seen as gifts whose use will eventually come under divine scrutiny. The writer reverts to this theme at the end of the poem (97–113) in lines whose syntax and thought echo and vary the statements at the beginning:

> Nis nu ofer eorþan   ænig monna
> mode þæs cræftig,   ne þæs mægeneacen,
> þæt hi æfre anum   ealle weorþen
> gegearwade,   þy læs him gilp sceððe,   100
> oþþe fore þære mærþe   mod astige,
> gif he hafað ana   ofer ealle men
> wlite ond wisdom   ond weorca blæd.
>
> *Gifts of men* 97–103

There is now no man on earth so skilful in mind or so powerful that all gifts are prepared for him alone, in case boasting should harm him, or his pride increase because of that honour, if he alone has beauty and wisdom and prosperity above all men.

The repetitive *þæs cræftig, þæs mægeneacen* recalls the first part of the earlier passage, while the remark about pride echoes the statement on pride in the second part, yet there is a difference, for the first man injures others by his pride, whereas the man in the final passage is saved by God from being injured himself. The list of talents which forms the central part of the poem must be seen within this framework in which men's relations with one another, through the gifts they receive from God, become the basis of their final relationship with God. Comprehensiveness is essential, so that any ability, even one as trivial as acrobatics, can be related to the service of God, but the reader is left to make this inference for himself.[8]

The poem *The fortunes of men*, like *The gifts of men*, is a hymn of praise, though the motives for praise and the over-all theme are very different. Whereas *The gifts of men* celebrates God's discretion in giving, linking it with his discretion in judging, *The fortunes of men* is concerned with order. As the poet says:

> Swa missenlice   meahtig dryhten
> geond eorþan sceat   eallum dæleð,
> scyreð ond scrifeð   ond gesceapo healdeð.
>
> *Fortunes of men* 64–6

So variously the mighty lord across the surface of the earth shares out to all, divides and decrees, and maintains the form of things.

This order, like that of *Maxims II* (50–55), is based on conflict for, as the author of *The order of the world* points out (82–5), one of God's acts of wisdom is to reconcile the opposites in his creation.[9] The main theme of *The fortunes of men* is man's helplessness. Parents may do their best to shelter their children but they are powerless against nature and its many ways of death (14).[10] The sad list of the blind, the lame, the exiled, the corpse swinging on the gallows and the drunkard in the hall, is bounded by two contrasting fates: at the beginning, the man who is killed in youth by the wolf (10–14) and at the end, the man who outlives youthful misery to reach a glad old age (58–63). As in *The gifts of men*, there is no over-all progression, but one or two themes provide a loose structure. The woman who weeps for the son

[8] Lines 82–4, cf Langland's reference to God's minstrels, *Piers Plowman*, B. ix, 102–3.
[9] See Ch. 4, pp. 61–2 and n. 19 above.
[10] cf T. A. Shippey, *Poems of wisdom and learning in Old English*, pp. 10–11.

who is eaten by the flames recalls the mother who mourns the son eaten by the wolf. More interesting is the connection of wolf and raven. These creatures are associated in heroic poetry with the battle-field, where they predict a glorious fate. Elsewhere they appear as impious desecrators of the human body, analogous to the worms and toads of Christian *contemptus* poetry such as *Soul and body I*: in *Maxims I* (146–51) the wolf is the treacherous companion of outlaws, who eventually kills and eats his friends, and in *Beowulf* (2447–9) the raven, like the raven of *The fortunes of men*, supplies the final degradation for the corpse on the gallows. The displacement of two of the conventional accompaniments of heroic battle scenes to unheroic or even anti-heroic settings adds to the air of futility engendered by the pathetic figure falling from the tree and the inglorious drunkard who dies by the sword on the mead-bench instead of on the battle-field. Whereas in heroic poetry death is a splendid thing, here it is a sign of failure and humiliation. In the second part of the poem these debased figures are replaced by symbols of success, the living figures of warriors, weapon-smiths, jewellers, harpists and falconers; the contrast between success and failure is the stronger because of the intrusion of heroic images such as wolf and raven, or death by the sword, into unheroic situations and modes of death. Yet for this poet, all fates are equally an expression not, as one might expect, of God's power, but of his merciful care for men. The sentiment is similar to that of *Maxims I* (29–34) where, in a curiously modern passage, death is presented as a divinely-ordained form of population control. The poet of *The fortunes of men* goes further, however, in seeing even death as an example of divine mercy, a conclusion which must have provoked his audience to further thought about the contents of the main part of the poem.[11]

In these two works on the gifts and fates of men the poet retains control over the poem's logical form by providing a framework within which to read it. In the *Maxims* the visible shape is even vaguer, and far more is left to the intuition of the audience. There are two collections of maxims: one in the Exeter Book, the other in one of the Cotton manuscripts (Tiberius B.i), preceding a copy of the *Anglo-Saxon Chronicle*. The Cotton *Maxims* (*Maxims II*) are often considered as a statement of what is permanent as against the changing events of the chronicle which follows them; the Exeter *Maxims* (*Maxims I*) are conceived as an exchange of wisdom, and in particular of the secret thoughts of the heart: as the poet says in the opening lines, *Gleawe men sceolon gieddum wrixlan* 'Wise men should exchange speeches'. They express, through the use of verbs such as *sceal* or *bið*, what is fitting, customary or characteristic in men and in the world around them,

---

[11] Theologically speaking, death is the supreme example of God's providence for it is through his determination of the moment of death, in relation to man's spiritual state, that God decides man's eternal destiny.

offering a body of general truths to which other poets can refer. The frequent echoes of these poems in works such as *Beowulf* and *The seafarer* suggest a taste for relating the particular to the general or the individual to the norm. Yet the gnomic poetry is more than a simple collection of quotable material: it has its own poetic value. *Maxims I* begins appropriately, after the call to an exchange of wisdom, with God and man's duty to praise him. The motive for praise is that life is a loan from God for which man must eventually account. This idea of life as something which is lent, a point more usually expressed by the adjective *læne* 'transitory' or 'loaned', is extended in *Maxims I* by a reminder of the great difference between man and God:

> Meotud sceal in wuldre,   mon sceal on eorþan
> geong ealdian.   God us ece biþ,
> ne wendað hine wyrda   ne hine wiht dreceþ,
> adl ne yldo   ælmihtigne;   10
> ne gomelað he in gæste,   ac he is gen swa he wæs,
> þeoden geþyldig.
>
> *Maxims I* 7–12

God must live in glory, man on earth must pass from youth to age. God is everlasting in comparison with us, events do not change him nor does anything, whether sickness or age, afflict the almighty: he does not grow old in spirit, but is always as he was, a patient lord.

Because our life is lent by God it is natural and inevitable that man should grow old, whereas God is untouched by those things which bring man to his end, the sickness and old age mentioned by the poet of *The seafarer* (70).

This opening section is completed by a reference to the vastness of God's creation, the different languages, lands and customs within which man lives; the rest of the poem explores the differences and similarities within God's world. Related statements are juxtaposed without any explicit grammatical connection, and the reader or listener is left to infer the relationship between ideas for himself. A statement about wisdom and justice is placed next to one on procreation, suggesting that the peace and unity which result from the exercise of wisdom are as inevitable and natural as the birth of children. Statements about birth and death frame a sentence on the falling of leaves from a tree, implying that both are part of the same natural order, and equally part of God's plan. Advice on how to educate children in order to ensure that they grow up resolute is followed by a

brief picture of stormy seas beating against the cliffs which provides
an image of the control necessary in the young man:

> Styran sceal mon strongum mode. Storm oft holm
> gebringeþ,
> geofen in grimmum sælum; onginnað grome fundian
> fealwe on feorran to londe, hwæþer he fæste stonde.
> Weallas him wiþre healdað, him biþ wind gemæne.
>
> *Maxims I* 50–53

A man should control himself with a firm mind. Often the sea
brings a storm, the ocean in grim seasons; from far off the yellow
waves begin to hurry, fierce towards the land, but it stands fast.
The cliffs stand firm against them; the wind is felt by both.

The two ideas are to be understood in relation to each other but the
connection is never clearly stated. In the following lines however the
related comparison between calm seas and human tranquillity is
unambiguous:

> Swa biþ sæ smilte,
> þonne hy wind ne weceð; 55
> swa beoþ þeoda geþwære, þonne hy geþingad habbað,
> gesittað him on gesundum þingum, ond þonne mid
> gesiþum healdaþ
> cene men gecynde rice.
>
> *Maxims I* 54–8

Just as the sea is calm when the wind does not wake it, so nations
are at peace when they have come to terms; they live in prosperity
and then bold men with their companions rule over their native
kingdom.

This unity between man and nature is one aspect of divine order; the
other, paradoxically, involves a parallel between man and God.
Whereas at the beginning of the poem it was their differences which
were emphasized, at the end the social structures created by man and,
in particular, the ceremonies of the hall, become a symbol of the
rewards of heaven:

> Hond sceal heofod inwyrcan, hord in streonum bidan,
> gifstol gegierwed stondan, hwonne hine guman gedælen.
> Gifre biþ se þam golde onfehð, guma þæs on heahsetle
> geneah;

lean sceal, gif we leogan nellað,   þam þe us þas lisse
geteode.

Maxims I 67–70

The hand shall be placed on the head, the treasure hoard wait in
its resting place, the gift-throne stand ready, when men share out
treasure. Greedy is he who receives that gold, the man on the high
seat will satisfy his desire, and, if we do not lie, there will be a
reward for us from the one who created these delights for us.

The poem which began with a statement of God's loan to man of life
ends with another 'loan': the transitory treasure-giving of this world
will be replaced by the treasure-giving of heaven, when man's desire
will truly be satisfied. The treatment of the word *lean*, with its ex-
ploitation of the different meanings of 'gift', 'loan' and 'reward',
recalls the treatment of the word *deman* in *The gifts of men*. In both
poems the underlying logic is inferred from the verbal paradox of the
opening and closing lines rather than from a succession of clearly
integrated statements.

The theme of this first part of the *Maxims* might be described as
order and contingency. The theme of the second part is also one of
order, but this time the emphasis is on change and contrast within the
world rather than on dependence on God. This second section, or
perhaps a second poem, begins with a series of statements about the
characteristics of the created world, the freezing and melting of frost
and fire, and the ice which bridges and shields the water. This bind-
ing and constricting power of nature is in turn subject to God who is
seen, typically, as unbinding the fetters of the frost to release the
natural turbulence of the waves. The theme of God controlling the
seasons is a commonplace of the writing of the period, the best-known
example being the description of the melting of the sword in the
under-water cave in *Beowulf*:

Þa þæt sweord ongan   1605
æfter heaþoswate   hildegicelum,
wigbil wanian.   Þæt wæs wundra sum,
þæt hit eal gemealt   ise gelicost,
ðonne forstes bend   fæder onlæteð,
onwindeð wælrapas,   se geweald hafað   1610
sæla ond mæla;   þæt is soð metod.

Beowulf 1605–11

Then that sword, the war-blade, began to melt in battle-icicles as
a result of the battle-blood. It was a great marvel that it melted
completely, just like ice when the Father unlooses the bond of

frost, untwists the water-fetters, he who has power over times and seasons; he is the true Lord.

After this opening passage on the seasons the poet turns to a related form of change: death, something often associated in Old English poetry with wintry cold. Here death, in contrast to the seasons, is something secret and hidden:

> Deop deadra wæg   dyrne bið lengest;
> holen sceal inæled,   yrfe gedæled
> deades monnes.   Dom biþ selast.
>
> *Maxims I* 78–80

The deep way of the dead is longest hidden; the lord shall be burned on the pyre, the property of the dead man divided. Reputation is best.[12]

As in the first section of the *Maxims* the comparison between the passage from life to death and the round of the seasons is implied rather than stated. The next group of sayings concerns men and women: the king and queen, the sailor with his Frisian wife, and the duties appropriate to these different social classes. The queen is to show the same qualities of cheerfulness, wisdom and liberality as the king, and to present the ceremonial cup in the hall; the sailor's wife is to wash her husband's clothes and remain loyal during his absences. After a brief section on sickness and murder the poet moves, via a statement on the usefulness of wisdom and the uselessness of evil to a final list of the things which are fitting in life, ornaments, music, battle and, at the end, the eucharist for holy men and sins for the heathen. The closing contrast between the idols which were the characteristic product of Odinn and the skies, which typify God's creation, brings the poet back to his starting point, namely God's control:

> Woden worhte weos,   wuldor alwalda,
> rume roderas;   þæt is rice god,
> sylf soðcyning,   sawla nergend,
> se us eal forgeaf   þæt we on lifgaþ,   135
> ond eft æt þam ende   eallum wealdeð
> monna cynne.   Þæt is meotud sylfa.
>
> *Maxims I* 132–7

Woden made idols, the almighty and glorious lord made the spacious skies; he is the powerful god, the true king himself, the

---

[12] *holen* is translated here as 'lord', cf *Wanderer* 31. If it is taken as 'holly' there is a further parallel with the natural world: man goes to the funeral pyre as holly to the fire.

saviour of souls who gave us all by which we live and who again at the end will rule over all mankind; he is the judge himself.

Whereas in the first part of the *Maxims* the key word was *lean*, here it is *metod*: God is the measurer who will measure man's fate just as he measured creation through his control of the seasons.[13] The third part of *Maxims I*, though based like parts one and two on a collection of loosely-linked generalizations, has an outer form as well as an inner one. At three points the normal metre is replaced by a group of short lines which mark the end of a section and divide the poem into four parts. The opening lines (138–40) assert the necessity for man to be wise, cheerful, praiseworthy and hard-working. The verb *onettan* in line 140 implies that man should stir himself, as it does in a similar passage in *Christ III*:

> Forðon sceal onettan,   se þe agan wile
> lif æt meotude,   þenden him leoht ond gæst
> somodfæst seon.
>
> *Christ* 1578–80

Therefore the man who wishes to win life from God must stir himself while light and spirit are together in him.

Elsewhere the word *onettan* is often used to describe the created world hastening towards its end. In *The seafarer* (49) both meanings are combined in the one sentence, for the world which comes to life in the spring is at the same time a warning to man to think of the end to which he, like the world, is hurrying. Similarly the man of *Maxims I* must be busy, for the day during which he can work (*dæges onettan*) will not last: as Christ said, 'As long as the day lasts I must carry out the work of the one who sent me; the night will soon be here when no one can work.' (John ix 4) It is within this context that the poem must be understood.

The general theme of section one (138–63) is friendship and the miseries of friendlessness, when man has to pass by villages unwelcomed and take as his companion the treacherous grey wolf. Friendship is linked in turn to possession: of a good horse, a bow and arrows and treasure. This modest prosperity, like the possession of friends, is seen as a mark of virtue, an idea expressed, typically, through a comparison with the natural world:

---

[13] The idea is similar to that which lies behind three late Anglo-Saxon manuscripts (Royal 1 E. vii, f. 1ᵛ, Tiberius C. vi, f. 7ᵛ, Vatican Regin. lat. 12, f. 68ᵛ) where God the creator is shown holding scales and dividers; see A. Heimann, 'Three illustrations from the Bury St Edmunds Psalter and their prototypes', *Journal of the Warburg and Courtauld Institutes* 29 (1966), pp. 39–59, especially pp. 46–56 and pls. 10–12.

Mæg god syllan
eadgum æhte   ond eft niman.
Sele sceal stondan,   sylf ealdian.
Licgende beam   læsest groweð.
Treo sceolon brædan   ond treow weaxan,
sio geond bilwitra   breost ariseð.
Wærleas mon ond wonhydig,
ætrenmod ond ungetreow,
þæs ne gymeð god.

Maxims I 155–63

God can give possessions to the fortunate man and take them away again. A hall stands and itself grows old. A tree which lies low grows least. Trees shall spread and faith increase, spring up in the breast of the merciful. As for the man who is faithless and foolish, poisonous-minded and untrue, God does not care for him.

When the poet says that the hall, the centre of heroic life, grows old (159) he implies that life itself, which is so often symbolized by the hall, passes, an echo of the idea expressed in the *onettan* of the opening lines. The unspoken parallel between the lazy man and the tree which produces little growth becomes explicit in the pun on *treo* and *treow*: faith will grow like a tree spreading its branches and the faithless man (*ungetreow*), who is not in harmony with the natural world, is also out of tune with God. Concord between men and between man and nature is seen to lead to peace with God.

Section two (164–80) unites the theme of wisdom, introduced in the opening three lines (138–40), with that of friendship, the two being linked through a reference to the gift of music. The passage ends with a picture of the warrior-brothers who fight and sleep together in a unity which only death can destroy (177–80). The next section, with its references to reproach, deceit and quarrelling (181–91), provides a transition from this harmonious picture to the final passage on the hostility and strife which have engaged mankind since the murder of Abel by Cain (192–204). The warlike courage praised in these final lines seems somewhat incongruous after the remark *ahogodan ond ahyrdon heoro slipendne* 'They invented and hardened the cruel sword' (200), yet there is a certain coherence in the poem. The three groups of short lines are all concerned in different ways with loyalty: the first asserts God's abhorrence of treachery (161–3), the second gives a picture of the power of friendship to resist mischievous speech (177–80) and the third affirms the importance of being on one's guard. In a world such as that described in the closing lines loyalty in war might well be seen as virtue with God as well as with man.

The shared wisdom of the *Maxims*, for all its apparent randomness, has an underlying form which distinguishes it from the riddling exchanges of *Solomon and Saturn*, which could have been extended indefinitely had the poet wished. The form however is only partly present in the text; it comes into being only when the reader supplies the connections which the poet has left unexpressed. This sharing of poetic creation implies a trust which could only have existed within a close-knit group with a common literary culture, for there is no suggestion that the poet expected the poem present in the audience's minds to differ from that in his own. It is a confidence which contrasts strangely with the normal authoritative stance of the poet, though both are equally derived from the fact of a shared tradition.

6 Narrative method

Most Old English narrative poetry other than *Beowulf* consists of biblical paraphrase and saints' lives. The form of these poems depends on the form of the originals from which they were translated or adapted rather than on the creative powers of their composers, and poetic art is absorbed into style rather than structure. The three Old Testament poems in Junius 11, for instance, differ in scope and purpose but none of them strays very far from the biblical narrative. The first poem consists of a close paraphrase of Genesis i–xxii 12, together with some introductory material on the creation and fall of the angels not found in the Bible. Interpolated into this poem is a six hundred line account of the rebellion and fall of the angels and of the temptation of Adam and Eve, translated into Old English from an Old Saxon poem of the second quarter of the ninth century: this interpolation is known as *Genesis B*. The narrative in *Genesis A* follows the Bible very closely, omitting some of the lists of names and adding small enlivening details, possibly derived from commentaries. The only major addition, apart from the introductory passage on the angels and the interpolated *Genesis B*, is an elaborate development of the story of the battle of the kings against Sodom (1960–2095). In the Bible the main emphasis of the story is on the names of the kings and of their kingdoms: the battle itself is barely mentioned. In the Old English poem this brief reference to the sacking of Sodom and Gomorrah, the capture of Lot, the pursuit by Abraham and the recovery of the captives is transformed into an energetic battle story in the heroic manner. As was said earlier, the poet marks this change by substituting for his normal appeals to the authority of books authenticating formulae such as *ic gefrægn*, *mine gefræge* and *we þæt soð magon secgan* which are usually associated with heroic poetry.[1] Both the vocabulary and the sentiments are those of poems like *Beowulf* and *The battle of Maldon*. The king of Elam, like Scyld, exacts tribute from the people of Sodom and Gomorrah; the warriors are equipped with the yellow shields, javelins and ring-patterned swords of Anglo-Saxon heroes; birds of prey tear the corpses; Abraham's friends, like Byrhtnoth's *comitatus*, promise to avenge his injury or to fall among the slain, and Abraham himself, like Byrhtnoth, gives war as a pledge instead of gold.

[1] See p. 36 above.

In contrast to the extended narrative of *Genesis A*, *Exodus* celebrates one incident from the Bible, the departure of the Israelites from Egypt, described in Exodus xiii and xiv. The poem combines a heroic description of the crossing of the Red Sea, the death of the pursuing Egyptians and the plundering of the dead by the victors, with a homiletic application in which this material is loosely linked to the lesson that man will reach heaven by obeying the Mosaic law. The opening lines of the poem, which interweave homiletic phrases like *gehyre se ðe wille* (7) with heroic formulae of the kind *we gefrigen habað* (1), define it as an example of moralized heroic. The predominant tone is warlike: Moses is described from the outset in military terms, while God is the lord of hosts whose gift to his followers is strength in fighting. Just as the poet of *Genesis A* enlarged and elaborated the account of the battle of the kings, so the poet of *Exodus* created from the restrained Bible narrative an exultant description of preparations for battle and of stormy death. But this vigorous and shapely account of flight and pursuit is not matched by its moral framework. The theme of obedience to the law, with which the poem opens, is taken up in the speech of Moses after the crossing of the Red Sea, when he reminds the Israelites that God will help them as long as they keep his laws (*Exodus* 558–64); the terrible death of the Egyptian army is a vivid reminder both to the Israelites and to the poet's audience of the power of God's promise, but it is never clearly linked to the matter of obedience. The passage in which the poet tries to show the relevance of his story to the Anglo-Saxon audience (517–48) is even less well articulated. The very tangible gains of the Israelites in the form of armour and ornaments won from the Egyptians bear little relationship to these lines on the well-worn topics of the passing joys of this world, the inevitability of God's judgment and the heavenly rewards to be expected by the righteous.

Daniel, like *Genesis A*, is a fairly straightforward paraphrase of the biblical text, with some omissions and expansions, though it shares with *Exodus* a homiletic purpose. The material has been redirected to some extent by presenting it in eye-witness terms and by interpreting the events described as a lesson against pride. Jerusalem is sacked as a punishment for the pride of the Israelites, Nebuchadnezzar's behaviour is consistently defined as *oferhygd*, and his son Belshazzar, equally filled with pride, draws down God's anger, rather as Satan does in *Genesis B*, through boasting that his armies are stronger than those of God. Whereas in *Exodus* story and moral never unite, here the narrative is well-adapted to the opening lesson: that no man should deprive God of any part of his love.

These three poems have been selected and arranged, either by the compiler of this manuscript or of a previous one, to form a single narrative sequence. Their section numbers run in one continuous series and this suggests that they were intended to be read as one, though the elaborate capitalization at the beginning of each poem shows that the scribe recognized that three separate poems were involved. The poems are linked by a number of passages which give the impression of continuity. Whereas the biblical Exodus began with a reference to the arrival in Egypt of the sons of Jacob, the Old English *Exodus* opens with a reference to the sons of Abraham, Jacob's grandfather, which provides a suitable link with the closing passage of *Genesis*, describing Abraham's sacrifice of Isaac. In the same way the poet of *Daniel* relates his account of the sack of Jerusalem by Nebuchadnezzar to the theme of *Exodus*, through a reference to the prosperity of the Israelites after Moses had led them out of Egypt. A subject which links all three poems is that of God's covenant with Abraham, described in *Genesis* 2188–215 and 2326–37, and mentioned briefly in Moses's speech after the crossing of the Red Sea (*Exodus* 558–62) and in the preliminaries to the sack of Jerusalem in *Daniel* 10. The same topic, of divine providence, is treated at length in *Exodus* 362–446, where the poet inserts an account of Noah's flood and of the sacrifice of Isaac into the middle of his description of the crossing of the Red Sea. It is unlikely that the Old English poems were composed with these relationships in mind, but there can be little doubt that their arrangement in the present manuscript, Junius 11, was intended to illustrate a single theme: God's redemptive plan. The main events and characters in the three poems are those invoked in the prayers for the dying, where God is asked to free the soul from all dangers as he freed Noah from the flood, Isaac from the hands of his father, Moses from the Egyptians, Daniel from the lions' den and the three children from the fiery furnace.[2] Moreover, the biblical material which forms the basis for these poems corresponds closely to the passages chosen for the Breviary readings for Lent and the readings for the Easter vigil service.[3] These liturgical readings were intended to show God's plan for the world as it developed in human history, and it seems likely that the arrangement of the poems in Junius 11 had a similar purpose. What is of interest is that the ordering of the poems as a group depends on an outside source just as much as the shape of each individual poem.

In the poems just discussed, the narrative progresses in strict chronological order, the only reshapings being the occasional expansions or reductions within this chronological progression and the asides and moralizing comments of the poets. In *Beowulf*, on the other hand,

---

[2] The full list of names is as follows: Enoch and Elijah, Noah, Abraham, Job, Isaac, Lot, Moses, Daniel, the three children, Susannah, David, Peter and Paul, Thecla.
[3] Gregory, *Liber responsalis*, *Patrologia latina* 78: 748–58, and *Liber sacramentorum*, *Patrologia latina* 78: 87–8; cf J. W. Bright, 'The relation of the Caedmonian *Exodus* to the liturgy', *MLN* 27 (1912), pp. 97–103, especially p. 101.

there is a complicated inter-weaving of events and allusions: some information about the hero is given quite late in the poem, and the Swedish and Geatish history which forms a kind of sub-plot to the poem is told piece-meal and out of order. The relationship between different events depends on juxtaposition in the text, not on chronology. In choosing to present his material in this way the poet incurred an obligation to guide his audience, directing their attention to relationships and reminding them of essential points. In addition, he gave an interpretation to his material. It is not simply a story told in an interesting and unusual way, but a critique of an ideal, and this is something which is conveyed through the structure of the poem rather than by authorial comment.

Most Old English poems start with a clear indication of the kind of work the audience should expect. The poet of *Exodus* indicates that his poem will have a homiletic purpose, and the poet of *Elene* creates the expectation of a carefully dated and authenticated historical document. In the same way the *Beowulf* poet, after his opening call for attention and his appeal to a shared experience, tells the audience to expect an aristocratic, heroic tale of the distant past, a time when the rules which govern normal historical events may not be relevant:

> Hwæt! We Gardena   in geardagum,
> þeodcyninga,   þrym gefrunon,
> hu ða æþelingas   ellen fremedon.
>
> *Beowulf* 1–3

Listen! we have heard of the glory of the kings of the people of the Spear-Danes in days gone by, how the princes did glorious deeds.

These lines raise expectations about subject matter, about values and about style, namely that the tale will be concerned with heroism and therefore, probably, with tragedy, that it will inculcate the values associated with kingship, that is courage, generosity and loyalty, and that it will be told with all the elaboration of heroic rhetoric. Having indicated the general scope of the poem, the poet swiftly outlines the early history of the Danish royal family from Scyld down to Hrothgar, who builds Heorot, the hall in which the first main action of the poem will take place. The poet's economy in establishing the main themes of his story can be seen in the figure of Scyld. This great king, whose glory it was to have reduced the surrounding tribes to paying tribute, had come mysteriously from over the sea, a helpless and destitute child; unlike most heroes he had no known ancestry and the fame he won depended on nature not on birth. There is here an indication that the poem will be concerned with nobility of a par-

ticular, individual kind, which was independent of family. In Scyld
and his son Beowulf the poet suggests some of the qualities required of
a king: Scyld was a great warrior, who made war on the neighbouring
tribes and increased his country's wealth through the tribute he
received; Beowulf's fame spread far and wide, so the poet implies,
because he was generous in youth and thus brought it about that his
people would support him in old age, when war came. The whole
poem will turn on these twin themes of the relationship between king
and people and the behaviour proper to youth and to age. The theme
of youth and age is developed in the lines on Scyld's funeral which
direct attention to the transitory nature of everything in this world,
even truly heroic lives, to the vast unknown outside the world and to
the probable tragic nature of the coming story. The description of the
funeral begins with a statement of inevitability: Scyld died *to gescæp-
hwile* 'at the appointed hour'. His departure was not only inevitable, it
was as mysterious as his arrival, for no one knew who received the
splendid cargo in the funeral ship. The darkness in which Scyld is
enveloped suggests at the very beginning of the poem the smallness of
the known world of hall, feasting and fighting, and the uncertainty
outside; it is a world in which monsters do not seem out of place and
where heroism must necessarily fail, however triumphant it is for a
time. Scyld left a son, and in his reference to him the poet hints at
another theme which will dominate the end of the poem: the tragedy
of a nation without a king. At this stage the audience is not asked to
advert to the fact that the poem will end with a funeral, as it began
with one, that Beowulf will die without an heir, leaving his country
open to attack, that Hygelac, who followed the same expansionist
policy as Scyld, will come to grief; these are parallels of which one is
aware only when the end of the poem is reached. What matters is that
the audience should be alert from the beginning to the issues which
will be raised.

The impression of transient glory, established in the description of
Scyld, is strengthened when the poet begins to set the scene for
Beowulf's first adventure, the killing of Grendel. Scyld's great grandson, Hrothgar, holds court in Heorot, a hall more splendid than had
ever been known before, and disposes of all that God gives him,
except for the communal land and men's lives. Like Scyld, Hrothgar
has been successful in subduing the tribes around him, and it is a safe
inference that he built Heorot to celebrate his victories; the fact that
the work of decorating it was imposed on many tribes suggests that it
was built from the tribute of subject peoples. But whereas Scyld's
glory ended only with his death and magnificent funeral, Hrothgar's
glory, symbolized by his hall, is less secure. As so often in the poem,
the poet creates a picture of worldly power and fame and then raises
doubts about the sufficiency of the world he has described:

Sele hlifade,
heah ond horngeap, heaðowylma bad,
laðan liges; ne wæs hit lenge þa gen
þæt se ecghete aþumsweorum
æfter wælniðe wæcnan scolde.

Beowulf 81-5

The hall towered up, high and wide-gabled; it awaited the surging
flames of hostile fire; the time had not yet come when the hostility
of father-in-law and son-in-law should awake as a result of deadly
enmity.

The prospect of human conflict is rejected, however, as abruptly as it
was introduced, and the poet turns instead to the unpredictable hostility of the non-human world outside the hall, with his reference to
Grendel, the *ellengæst* who lives in darkness, envying the light from
which he is excluded.

In these first two sections of the poem, lines 1–114, the poet has
indicated the themes that will be treated in the poem, and has raised
expectations of a poem of a particular kind, heroic, but involving a
questioning of the values of the world he portrays. It is a world set like
a small point of light in a vast and evil darkness, whose happiness is
fragile, where heroes die in the prime of life, splendid halls are burned
down, and marriages end in family feuds.

The ending of *Beowulf* which, exceptionally for an Old English
poem, is as well-fashioned as the beginning, echoes the themes of its
opening sections. In Beowulf the Dane the poet drew attention to one
of the basic ideals of heroic society, loyalty—the generosity of the lord
and the reciprocal duty of the retainer—linking this to the theme of
youth and age. At the end of the poem the other Beowulf, Beowulf the
Geat, lies dead, watched over by Wiglaf, and when his followers
emerge from the wood to see what has happened they are greeted by
Wiglaf's contemptuous speech: 'The man who wishes to speak the
truth may say that the lord who gave you those treasures, the equip-
ment in which you stand there, completely threw away that war-
gear. . . . Death is better for any man than a life of shame.' The poet
had asserted that it was a universal principle that generosity would be
repaid, but in Beowulf's case this is not so: he had been liberal to his
followers but 'in age, when war comes' they deserted him. It was said
of the first Beowulf, *lof-dædum sceal in mægþa gehwære man geþeon* and of
Beowulf the second that he was *lof-geornost*; but although he has lived
up to the ideal, society has not equalled him. Life is shown not to
conform to what is supposedly universal, fitting and inevitable. That
the poet intends no criticism of Beowulf himself is clear from the

closing lines of the poem in which he characterizes the eulogy by the hero's followers as something entirely fitting:

> Eahtodan eorlscipe   ond his ellenweorc
> duguðum demdon,   swa hit gedefe bið
> þæt mon his winedryhten   wordum herge,
> ferhðum freoge,   þonne he forð scile
> of lichaman   læded weorðan.

Beowulf 3173-7

They praised his greatness and his mighty deeds, gave a noble judgment on him, as it is fitting that a man should praise his friend and lord in his words, love him in his heart, when he has to go forth from the body.

Beowulf is always portrayed as the supreme hero: he is pleased to have killed the dragon and to have won the treasure for his people, and he comforts himself at the moment of death with the thought that he has lived a good life. He has been a strong ruler, just and honourable, defending his own, but refraining from attacking others; his passing from life is eased by the sight of the treasures he has gained. Some readers have seen in this sentiment a hint of avarice, but the poet offers no word of blame. Instead, he shows the splendour of the ideal by which Beowulf has lived, but places it side by side with a reality to which it is irrelevant. The naked truth is heard in the long speech of the messenger, announcing to the watchers on the headland the death of their lord and of their nation. He recalls the long history of war against Swedes and Merovingians, and the fact that only Beowulf has stood between the Geats and destruction; clearly, Wiglaf is no adequate substitute, and as for the treasure, it is good only for the pyre. There is here, in the simple juxtaposition of ideas, a hard judgment on conventional heroism. The verdict is the more successful for being given not by the poet himself—who can continue to express unqualified admiration—but by the impersonal public voice of the messenger, the chorus to the poem.

Just as *Beowulf* excels most Old English poems by having an end as well as a beginning, so, in contrast to the Christian narrative poems discussed, it has a clearly articulated structure apart from the simple story. As is well known, the poem is disposed in terms of a contrast between youth and age, between the rising and the setting of the hero's life. The first two episodes show the youthful retainer, making a name for himself and then returning home having proved his worth, to be rewarded by lands on which he can settle down; the last episode shows the old king, with the opposing duty of protecting his people, still acting the part of the hero even though his strength is inadequate to the task. This contrast is apparent only at the end of the poem; it is our abstraction. We do not know at the beginning, when we first encounter Beowulf in the Grendel episode, that this is to be contrasted with the later dragon episode, though when we come to the dragon episode the poet invites us to look back and compare Beowulf's behaviour then with what happened earlier. It must be remembered, however, that the structure is not something static which can be observed all at one time: on the contrary, its effect is cumulative and constantly shifting.

The poem falls into three distinct sections: the fight against Grendel (1–1250), the fight against Grendel's mother (1251–2199), and the dragon-fight (2200–3182). It is possible that it was recited in three instalments, for there is a clear break in the narrative between each episode and the next, followed by a brief summary of earlier events which serves to remind listeners of what has gone before. A poem which is constructed around three rather similar exploits must offer variety, otherwise it will seem repetitive; moreover, the tasks themselves must increase in difficulty to avoid any feeling of anti-climax. The problem is greatest in the first two sections, where the hero defeats, one after the other, two sub-human man-eating creatures, both of whom have attacked Hrothgar's hall. The first fight, that against Grendel, is described largely in chronological order and with few digressions. Having set the scene through his description of the building of Heorot, the poet introduces the protagonists. He gives a brief outline of Grendel's first visit to Heorot, his murder of thirty warriors, his repeated attacks over twelve years, and the helplessness against him of the Danes. He then turns to Beowulf, describing his journey to Denmark, his interviews with the coastguard and the door-keeper, and finally his encounter with Hrothgar himself. Much of this part of the poem is concerned with establishing the hero as someone worthy of his role. Whereas Grendel is characterized in both religious and secular terms, as an outcast from the joys of heroic society and as a descendant of Cain and therefore an outcast from the joys of Christian society, Beowulf is defined in a strictly secular way. He identifies himself as son of Ecgtheow and thane of Hygelac and to this Hrothgar adds the information that he was the grandson of Hrethel. It is true that Hrothgar looks on him as sent by God but Beowulf himself makes no claim to divine favour: when he makes his long retort to Unferth for instance it is clear that he places his trust in his own strength and in the course of events. Beowulf's greatness is established by showing him in conversation with a variety of characters. In his speeches to the coastguard and to Wulfgar he shows himself modest, courteous, yet fully confident of his own powers; they in turn are immediately conscious of his distinction. His opening speech to Hrothgar, in which he supports his request to be allowed to fight

Grendel by mentioning some of his youthful exploits against monsters, is convincing partly because it has been preceded by Hrothgar's recollections of Beowulf's father, and his confirmation that Beowulf's reputation was already well known. Hrothgar's reminiscences about the events which had brought Ecgtheow to his court, and of his own role in settling the feud, place the hero within a great network of family relationships, making it clear that he is no mere adventurer, but an accepted member of an aristocracy linked by ties of marriage and loyalty. The attack by Unferth enhances Beowulf's reputation first because it is provoked by jealousy of a hero greater than himself and secondly because it provides Beowulf with a further opportunity to give his credentials as a fighter of monsters.

The poet's next task is to prepare the audience for the fight itself. The early references to Grendel have given a rather vague impression of his depredations. The audience knows that he attacks at night, that his attacks have reduced the Danish warriors to sleeping ignominiously in the outbuildings instead of in the hall, and that those few warriors who have tried to fight him have disappeared, leaving only the bloodstained benches as a witness. The poet now needs to create a more intense apprehension of evil. The banquet scene with its ceremonies and speeches ends with the departure of Hrothgar who knows not only that attack is imminent but that Grendel has been brooding over it from daybreak until nightfall. This deliberate, meditated intentness transforms Grendel into something far more menacing than the simple man-eater of earlier scenes. The same slow deliberation marks the poet's description of events leading up to the attack. The preparations of the Geats are almost leisurely as Beowulf removes his armour and together with his warband lies down in the hall. There is no sudden descent by the monster but instead a slow, stalking approach through the darkness. The poet constantly breaks the narrative, shifting his attention from monster to hall and back again, until finally Grendel breaks down the door and the pace of events changes. The poet signals this change through a series of words denoting haste, in particular the adverbs *sona* and *hraþe*, but at the same time he creates an almost painful suspense as Grendel gloats over the expected feast and Beowulf watches motionless. This capacity to stretch the action appears above all in the description of the fight itself, where the poet creates the impression of a prolonged struggle by detailing the thoughts and feelings of his characters rather than their actions. The fight once over he returns to his earlier style, expanding his narrative with lengthy speeches, a careful description of ceremonies and treasures, and two subsidiary narratives (those of Sigemund and Finnsburg) with which the company in the poem is entertained.

The second episode retains this amplitude of manner, but does so in

parallel with the earlier sections, exploiting the details and information given there. The feast at which Grendel's death is celebrated,
and which ends with the attack by Grendel's mother, is to a large
extent a repeat of the feast on the previous evening, immediately after
Beowulf's arrival. Such set pieces are frequent in heroic poetry, but in
Beowulf the repeats are used to develop expectations aroused earlier in
the poem, not simply as an aid to composition. Grendel's first attack
(115–25) was made on a group of warriors asleep after a feast,
oblivious of the dark fate of men; his second attack (702 ff) takes place
after a series of specific actions by people in the hall: Wealhtheow
carries round the cup, Hrothgar leaves the hall and the warriors lie
down to sleep. The audience knows, because the poet tells them, that
Grendel will attack the hall. The attack and the events which precede
it are linked in their minds almost as though one is the consequence of
the other; when, therefore, the poet repeats the same pattern of events
in his account of the feast after Grendel's death the audience expects a
similar outcome. Wealhtheow moves through the hall presenting the
cup, the hall is cleared of benches, the bedding is spread out and the
warriors lie down to sleep. They expect nothing. The audience, aware
of no monster other than Grendel, is yet uneasily conscious of the
parallel with the earlier feast. But whereas on that occasion they knew
what would happen, this time the threat is undefined and the anxiety
is therefore greater. The contrast between the heedless warriors and
their audience is intensified by a series of verbal echoes and implied
comparisons. The following lines recall the reference at the beginning
of the poem to the warriors sleeping in the hall, as well as the description of Hrothgar retiring to bed after the feast to welcome Beowulf:

> Wyrd ne cuþon,
> geosceaft grimme, swa hit agangen wearð
> eorla manegum, syþðan æfen cwom
> ond him Hroþgar gewat to hofe sinum,
> rice to ræste.
>
> *Beowulf* 1233–7

They did not know the course of events, grim destiny, such as had
come to many nobles after evening came and Hrothgar went to
his room, the mighty one to his bed.

The line in which the poet comments that the warriors slept in the
hall *swa hie oft ær dydon* revives the memory of what had equally often
followed their action; the allusion to the warrior *fus ond fæge* hints at a
further death without revealing in any way how this will come about.
In such a context the approving description of the Danes as always
ready for an attack seems ironic indeed.

If the poem was recited in three parts, as has been suggested, this would be a splendid point at which to pause. The lines which immediately follow seem to confirm this view for the details of Grendel's attack, defeat and death and the repeated reference to the doomed warrior would hardly have been necessary in a continuous recitation, whereas they would provide a convenient reminder of earlier events to an audience which was listening to the story in instalments:

> Sum sare angeald
> æfenræste,   swa him ful oft gelamp,
> siþðan goldsele   Grendel warode,
> unriht æfnde,   oþþæt ende becwom,
> swylt æfter synnum.

Beowulf 1251–5

One paid dearly for his night's rest, as often happened after Grendel occupied the gold hall and accomplished evil, until an end came, death after his sins.

It is at this point that the poet first reveals the existence of Grendel's mother, in words which echo those used earlier of her son. Both are descended, appropriately, from Cain, and here, as before, the poet expands this point into an account of the death of Abel, the banishment of Cain and the descent from him of all monsters. Yet there is one difference: whereas Grendel lived in the shadows, his mother inhabits the cold waters. This introductory passage is typical of the way in which the second episode is told, through recall and variation. Both episodes include a description of a journey out to the monsters' lake: the first journey is taken in joyful mood, following the tracks of the dying monster to a lake welling with that same monster's blood; on the second occasion the trail is of a monster who bears with her one of Hrothgar's thanes, and the lake is bloodstained from his death. Whereas the first fight is preceded by an account of Beowulf handing his armour to an attendant, the fight against Grendel's mother requires full war-gear, and the poet emphasizes the point by providing a detailed description of the coat of mail, shining helmet and pattern-welded sword with which Beowulf protects himself. The comparative ease with which Beowulf overcame Grendel is contrasted with the difficulties of the second, underwater contest, where at one point he seems to be at his opponent's mercy, and kills her only with the help of a magic sword found in the cave itself. The most interesting example of formal parallelism however comes after the fight. The victory is followed and celebrated, as was the earlier one, by a feast. After the speeches are over the poet repeats the details which he had used twice before to signal a night attack: it grows dark,

Hrothgar retires, Beowulf goes to sleep, the hall towers up, and because these statements have acquired associations with evil the audience half expects a third monster to appear. This time, however, expectation is disappointed and the warriors wake to a fine and sunny morning.

This second episode ends with the return of Beowulf to his home, something which has no parallel in episode one, and which to some readers seems weak and repetitive, particularly in its re-telling of the happenings at Heorot. The narrative is skilfully contrived, however, and includes many details not given in the earlier parts of the poem, for instance Grendel's glove, the name of the Geat who was killed, the pedigree of the treasures given to Beowulf by Hrothgar and the story of Freawaru. The episode ends with the hero triumphant, having proved his worth and received the due reward of sword and ancestral lands. At this point the third episode begins, the break in narrative being marked by a brief summary of the fifty-year interval between Beowulf's return home and his encounter with the dragon.

Despite this marked chronological break, the third episode is carefully linked to the previous two. The dragon fight is twice compared to the fight against Grendel: on the first occasion the poet notes that Beowulf had survived many battles during the years between the two fights and explains that this is why he scorned to lead an army against the dragon (2345–54); on the second, Beowulf himself justifies his wearing armour against the dragon and recalls the very different encounter with Grendel, when he had relied solely on his grip (2518–24). In an earlier speech he outlines his life from the age of seven, when he was entrusted by his father to his grandfather king Hrethel, up to the disastrous Frisian expedition in which his uncle Hygelac was killed. This raid is described four times in the poem and marks the turning point between the earlier and later parts of the story. It is first mentioned in the description of the feast after the death of Grendel. Towards the end of the festivities Wealhtheow walks through the hall carrying the ceremonial cup and, having offered it first to Hrothgar, turns to Beowulf. Like her husband she presents him with gifts: two bracelets and a neck-ring. In both cases, the treasures are distinguished by one of the poet's authenticating phrases, but whereas the armour is praised for its excellent workmanship, here the focus is on future history. The necklace is not only the most splendid since the necklace of the Brosings: it was worn by Hygelac in his last battle, and after his death it became the property of the Franks. The account of the necklace, like other digressions in the poem, increases the impression of leisurely grandeur; it has in addition a structural function. The immediate context of the passage is the forebodings of Wealhtheow about the succession to the Danish throne. Hrothgar's *scop* has recited the tragic tale of Finnsburg and the poet returns to the situation in Heorot: in one part of the hall Hrothgar and Hrothulf sit side by side with Unferth at their feet; further down the bench Beowulf is placed between the king's young sons, Hrethric and Hrothmund. The poet comments on the trust and loyalty existing between the king, his nephew and his *þyle*, suggesting by this very assertion a doubt about the future. This doubt is intensified by Wealhtheow when she urges Hrothgar to leave the throne to his sons and protests her faith in Hrothulf's good will towards his cousins. In this context there is a chilling quality about the statement that the necklace presented by Wealhtheow to Beowulf was to be worn by Hygelac in his last battle. The reference is the more striking because until this moment Hygelac has been presented as the one stable point in the poem. Beowulf's proud references to his position as Hygelac's thane and his desire to have his armour returned to his lord in the event of his death establish Hygelac in the audience's minds not simply as a great lord but as a figure of permanence in a world where death can come even to a hero. The sudden leap forward to a time when Hygelac is dead suggests as perhaps nothing else could the precarious basis of human trust. When, six hundred lines later, Beowulf confidently affirms that Hygelac will help the Danes against attack and that Hrethric will always find friends among the Geats, the audience could hardly fail to note the contrast between expectation and reality.

The other references to the Frisian expedition come in the final episode of the poem, which is placed in the period after Hygelac's death. Beowulf is now king, yet loyalty to Hygelac continues to provide the motivation for his actions. In youth his constant desire had been to act so as to deserve the praise of his lord; in age he habitually looks back, trying to remain true to the same ideal. Just as he had refused to use a sword against Grendel, believing that this would increase his reputation with his lord, so when he decides to use a sword against the dragon he does so within the context of his long service to Hygelac, when he fought before him in the army and repaid his gifts *leohtan sweorde*:

> Symle ic him on feðan   beforan wolde,
> ana on orde,   ond swa to aldre sceall
> sæcce fremman,   þenden þis sweord þolað,
> þæt mec ær ond sið   oft gelæste.
> Syððan ic for dugeðum   Dæghrefne wearð
> to handbonan,   Huga cempan.
>
> *Beowulf* 2497–2502

I used always to fight before him in the troop, alone in the fore-front, and shall always do the same, for as long as this sword endures, which has often and at all times served me since I killed Dæghrefn, the Frankish champion, before the retainers.

The one fight which stands out in Beowulf's mind is that in which his lord died, fifty years before, and his own death against the dragon is, emotionally if not factually, a final act of retainership rather than a conscious act of kingship. This loyalty to a dead lord adds to the sad inevitability with which he goes to his death: owing allegiance to the dead, what can he do but die. As he says himself:

> Ealle wyrd forsweop
> mine magas   to metodsceafte,
> eorlas on elne;   ic him æfter sceal.

Beowulf 2814–16

Events have swept away all my kinsmen to their appointed fate, the nobles in their strength; I must follow them.

For his followers the fullness of the tragedy is expressed by the messenger in a further allusion to Hygelac's unprovoked attack on Frisia which, together with the far older feud against the Swedish royal house, will now bring renewed fighting.

This expectation of hostility from the Swedes is strange, for the reigning king is Eadgils, who owed a debt of gratitude to the Geats for sheltering him in exile, and to Beowulf in particular for helping him regain his throne. The complexity of the situation is seen in the figure of Wiglaf, the youthful retainer who is the heir to Beowulf's heroic aspirations as well as to his armour. Beowulf and Wiglaf are related, for both are members of the Wægmundings, yet Wiglaf's father had fought on the Swedish side in the attack in which Heardred was killed, and it is the sword which he won from Eanmund in that fight which Wiglaf now uses to help Beowulf against the dragon. In retaliation for the death of Heardred Beowulf helped Eanmund's brother, Eadgils, regain the Swedish throne, but now the old hero who had once been accepted in adoptive sonship by Hrothgar, the brother-in-law of Onela, and who had later fought against Onela, leaves his armour to Wiglaf, whose father had served Onela and had, in the process, killed Beowulf's lord.

These historical details help to confer dignity on the folk-hero from whom Beowulf derives, and create the impression of a unified web of events against which the three monster-killings take place. But they do more than this: they provide a means of judging the values portrayed in the story as a whole. The main thread of *Beowulf* is concerned with glorifying an ideal: Beowulf himself is a great figure in the heroic tradition. He has followed the advice given him by

Hrothgar, has profited by the example of Heremod and has avoided both arrogance and avarice. The poet defines him as a heroic king (2390) in words used also of Scyld and Hrothgar, but not, interestingly, of Hygelac. His retainers see no fault in him when they lament his death, save only that he was too determined to hold on to his great destiny (3084). Yet in his death he demonstrates the failure of the principle enunciated at the beginning of the poem: that the result of courage and generosity is loyalty. This failure comes about because life is not like literature. Beowulf himself is a mythical figure: he is related to historical characters but he is not himself historical; he participates in historical events but is portrayed by the poet only in his encounters with monsters. Side by side with this mythical figure the poet places historical reality: the stories of Heremod, Finnsburg, and of Freawaru in the earlier part of the poem and the deaths of the Swedish and Geatish kings and of their families in the later part. The picture is almost entirely tragic and the tragedy springs from an adherence to the heroic ideals of loyalty and vengeance which are so praised in the main part of the story. Heroism may be a glorious thing in poetry but in real life it is seen to lead to nothing but misery. Moreover, by juxtaposing the mythical Beowulf, a type of the heroic ideal, with the real life events of the digressions the poet has shown the ideal for what it is: something splendid but unpractical. When, eventually, ideal and reality meet, reality (in the shape of the hero's age and the cowardice of ordinary men) is shown to be inadequate to the demands of the heroic situation.

7 Rhythm and style

Old English poetry, whether it was intended for private reading or for public reading or recitation, depended for its poetic effect on rhythmic and alliterative patterns rather than on its shape on the manuscript page. It may be assumed therefore that poets—at least the more skilful ones—would have exploited rhythm for poetic effect just as they exploited the other resources of their art. If one reads the poetry aloud it becomes clear that Anglo-Saxon poets differed considerably in their choice of rhythms, and also that individual poets associated different rhythmic patterns with different meanings. Of course, the interpretation of Old English verse patterns is to some extent a subjective matter, and this must have been as true of performance in the Anglo-Saxon period as it is today. There are however distribution patterns on which most readers would agree.

In the discussion which follows, metrical patterns will be identified according to the five types associated with the name of Eduard Sievers.[1] Some use will be made of the modifications to Sievers's system introduced by Bliss and Cable, but for the sake of simplicity and clarity the sub-divisions of the five types will be ignored.[2] One important point follows from the choice of Sievers's system rather than that of Pope. Not only will the lines vary in length; their aesthetic effect will be different. In Pope's system each half-line occupies the same amount of time as the others. It follows therefore that a half-line with only four syllables, such as *Grendel gongan* (711), will be said more slowly than a half-line with nine, and will appear to slow the verse down, whereas half-lines such as *sypðan he hire folmum æthran* (722) will appear to move more rapidly. In a system with variable

---

[1] E. Sievers, 'Zur Rhythmik des germanischen Alliterationsverses I', *Beiträge zur Geschichte der deutschen Sprache und Literatur* 10 (1885), pp. 209–314 and *Altgermanische Metrik*. The five types are as follows:

$$A \mid \times \mid \times ; B \times \mid \times \mid ; C \times \mid\mid \times ; D \mid\mid \setminus \times ; E \mid \setminus \times \mid$$

[2] A. J. Bliss, *The metre of Beowulf*; T. Cable, *The meter and melody of Beowulf*; see also J. C. Pope, *The rhythm of Beowulf*. Sievers and Bliss emphasize stress, whereas Pope emphasizes rhythm and Cable argues for the importance of melody. The three systems are not entirely incompatible, and I have drawn to some extent on Pope's work though, for reasons which there is not space to discuss here, I do not accept a strictly isochronous system, or the necessity for initial rests marked by a note from the harp.

line-length the result will be exactly opposite: half-lines with only four syllables will seem to make the verse speed up, while longer half-lines will create a more lingering effect. It must be remembered however that Sievers's five types provide only a very inadequate shorthand for describing the metre: rhythm involves far more than the arrangement of stress-patterns defined by Sievers's classification. Variations in word division and phrasing can create quite different effects within a single stress-pattern. The length of particular syllables and the number of syllables to the line—both of which can vary considerably without altering the underlying metre—can alter the pace of the verse. The pauses which result from some combinations of patterns bring about emphases which are independent of stress. In addition, individual performances must have differed. Yet even with the simple five-type classification it is possible to show connections between rhythm and meaning and to offer an objective basis for one kind of stylistic comment.

Analysis of the metre of *Beowulf* has shown that the patterns which occur most frequently are Sievers's types A, B, and D.[3] 84 per cent of the lines consist of an A-type half-line combined with a half-line of another type, the preferred combinations being A + B and D + A, as in the following two lines:

A	féasceaft funden	hé þæs frofre gebad	B	7
D	léof landfruma	lange ahte	A	31

The A-type rhythm therefore predominates and other rhythmic patterns can be seen as departures from this basic rhythm, either for the sake of variety or to produce specific effects. Much of this chapter will be concerned with changes in the proportions and combinations of these different rhythmic patterns.

Old English poetry, like that of any other period, involves an interplay between metre and normal speech rhythm, and between speech units based on the verse line and those based on clauses or sentences. The underlying metre is that of a sequence of A-type half-lines; it is maintained by ensuring that about half the total number of half-lines are of this type, so that there is an alternation between normal and displaced rhythms. Because the poetry is basically an oral form, not a written one, recognition of the line division depends on features

---

[3] The actual numbers (based on Bliss's tables, *Metre of Beowulf*, pp. 135–38) are as follows:

A 2902; B 941; C 547; D 1356; E 556

For the combinations into lines see Bliss, Table II, p. 136.

detectable by ear, namely a rhythm which creates a fractional pause at the end of each line and an alliterative system which indicates which half-lines are paired; in addition there is a preference for beginning a line with an A-type unit, which draws attention to the line structure as well as reasserting the underlying metre. Sentence structure, which involves occasional run-on lines and pauses at the midline, is set against this regular line division. Some of the main features of this interplay between syntax and verse-form can be seen in the following passage taken from the opening section of *Beowulf*:

C	Oft Scyld Scefing → *sceaþena þreatum*,	A
A	*monegum mægþum* → meodosetla ofteah, #	E 5
A	*egsode eorlas*. # Syððan ærest wearð #	B
A	*feasceaft funden*, # he þæs frofre gebad, #	B
A	*weox under wolcnum*, → weorðmyndum þah,	E
#	oðþæt him æghwylc → þara ymbsittendra	D
#	ofer hronrade → *hyran scolde*,	A 10
A	*gomban gyldan*. # Þæt wæs god cyning! #	C
B	Ðæm eafera wæs # *æfter cenned*,	A
A	*geong in geardum*, # þone god sende	C
A	*folce to frofre*; → fyrenðearfe ongeat	E
C	þe hie ær drugon → *aldorlease*	A 15
A	*lange hwile*. # Him þæs liffrea,	C
A	*wuldres wealdend*, → woroldare forgeaf; #	E
A	*Beowulf wæs breme* → (blæd wide sprang),	D
A	*Scyldes eafera* → Scedelandum in. #	E
C	Swa sceal geong guma → *gode gewyrcean*	A 20
D	fromum feohgiftum→ on fæder bearme,	C

þæt hine on ylde → *eft gewunigen*⁀   A

A   *wilgesiþas,* # þonne wig cume,⁀   C

A   *leode gelæsten;* → lofdædum sceal⁀   E

A   *in mægþa gehwære* → man geþeon.[4]   A   25

Points of particular note are the way in which a fractional pause at
the end of a line is created by a B or E-type half-line followed by an
A-type beginning with a stressed syllable (5, 6, 7, 17), whereas in
similar combinations with an unstressed syllable at the beginning of
the second line the rhythm runs on (24/25). Pauses are also created by
following an A or D-type half-line with a B or C-type which begins
with two lightly-stressed syllables (6, 7, 11, 13, 16, 23); if the second
unit begins with only one lightly-stressed syllable, on the other hand,
the line runs on (21). Sometimes these rhythmical pauses coincide
with syntactic ones and reinforce them; sometimes they occur at inter-
mediate points in a sentence and draw attention to some phrase
requiring emphasis. Because of the preference for beginning a line
with an A-type unit, sense-groups ending at the mid-line tend to end
with an A-type cadence whereas sense-units which coincide with the
end of the line show more variety. In total, however, there is a strong
preference for ending a sense-group with a lightly-stressed syllable
(i.e. A, C or D); when a sense-group ends with a B or E-type half-line
it is usually associated with a point needing special emphasis. For
instance the general comment on Scyld's funeral, his fate and, by
implication, the fate of other men, which sums up the first section of
the poem, ends with a B-type half-line:

Men ne cunnon

secgan to soðe,   selerædende,   D

hæleð under heofenum,   hwa þæm hlæste onfeng.   B

                                                                        50–52

This provides an appropriately definite ending to the passage and

---

[4] Throughout this chapter A-type half-lines are set in italic and the pattern of other
lines is indicated in the margin, except for light half-lines which are left unmarked. The
rhythm is set out in full only where this is necessary to an understanding of the
commentary. The symbol # is used for a pause in the rhythm and the symbol → for
continuous rhythm. The term 'sense-group' is used of sentence divisions ending with a
full-stop or semi-colon in the ASPR edition; the word 'cadence' refers to the rhythmic
pattern ending such a group.

draws attention to the generalization. Other examples of general comments which end with or consist of a B-type half-line are Beowulf's two statements about destiny:

Gǽð á wyrd swá hío scel 455

Wyrd oft nereð

E   unfǽgne eorl,   þonne his ellen deah.   B

572-3

Elsewhere, the comments which serve to sum up a character or event are treated in the same way, for instance the comment on Heremod which serves to distinguish him from Beowulf,

hine fyren onwod 915

or that on Hildeburh,

þæt wæs geomuru ides 1075

or on Hama's exploits,

geceas ecne ræd 1201

or the comment on the dead Æschere,

swylc Æschere wæs 1329

Whereas B-type cadences seem to be emphatic, E-type ones seem to have some different association. Two sense-units in the opening section of the poem which end with an E-type half-line precede a general comment and this may perhaps be important (19b, 50a).[5]

The poet's skill in varying his rhythmic patterns can be seen particularly clearly in the description of Beowulf's fight with Grendel and of the preliminaries to it (662–836). The first few lines, telling of Hrothgar's departure from the hall, have a normal narrative rhythm:

B   Ða him Hroþgar gewat   mid his hæleþa gedryht,   B

D   eodur Scyldinga,   *ut of healle*;

---

[5] On the pauses and cadences in *Beowulf* 1–52 see M. Daunt, 'Some modes of Anglo-Saxon meaning', in *In memory of J. R. Firth*, pp. 66–78, especially pp. 73–5. Parts of the present chapter are an attempt to develop the ideas suggested in this article.

D   wolde wigfruma   *Wealhþeo secan,*

    cwen to gebeddan.

662–5

When the poet reaches the mention of the watch against Grendel however the rhythm changes:

Hæfde kyningwuldor

    Grendle togeanes,   *swa guman gefrungon,*

E   seleweard aseted;   sundornytte beheold   E

C   ymb aldor Dena,   eotonweard abead.   E

665–8

The cluster of E-type half-lines provides a striking contrast in rhythm to the repeated A-type of line 666 and draws attention to the statement that a guard had been set. The next few lines (669–76), describing Beowulf's trust in God, reestablish the underlying A-type rhythm. Then comes an eleven-line speech by Beowulf which retains this underlying A-type rhythm but with a subtle change: normally the most frequent combinations are of A-type half-lines with B or D-type ones, but here there is an exceptionally high proportion of C-type half-lines, only one D-type and no E-types:

    No ic me an herewæsmun   *hnagran talige,*

    guþgeweorca,   þonne Grendel hine;   C

    forþan ic hine sweorde   *swebban nelle,*

    aldre beneotan,   þeah ic eal mæge.   C   680

    Nat he þara goda   þæt he me ongean slea,   C

    rand geheawe,   þeah ðe he rof sie   C

    niþgeweorca;   ac wit on niht sculon   C

    secge ofersittan,   gif he gesecean dear   B

    wig ofer wæpen,   ond siþðan witig god   B   685

B   on swa hwæþere hond,   *halig dryhten,*

                  × ×   × / / ×
mærðo deme,   swa him gemet þince.   C

                                                    677–87

The absence of the asymmetrical D and E-type rhythms and the high proportion of C-type half-lines with their adjacent stresses gives an impression of stability to these lines. The same rhythmic features characterize Beowulf's speech of encouragement to Hrothgar after the attack by Grendel's mother (1384–96) and the speech he makes before diving into the lake (1474–91), and it is notable that in all three cases he is concerned with inspiring confidence in his hearers.

The lines describing Grendel's relentless advance on the hall, by contrast, have fewer C-type half-lines than normal, and this is to be expected, for these lines convey apprehension rather than stability. What is of interest here however is the poet's use of emphatic cadences and end-stopped lines. As was said earlier, the *Beowulf* poet normally ends a sense-group with a lightly-stressed syllable, and tends to pause at the mid-line rather than at the end of a line.[6] In the twenty-three lines beginning *com on wanre niht* (702b–724a) seven of the twelve breaks occur at the end of a line and five at the mid-line; of the seven end-stopped lines, four end with a strongly-stressed syllable (711, 713, 719, 722):

Ða com of more   under misthleoþum   710

                          /   \ × /
Grendel gongan,   godes yrre bær;   E

mynte se manscaða   *manna cynnes*

                       × / × /
sumne besyrwan   in sele þam hean.   B

Wod under wolcnum   to þæs þe he winreced,

goldsele gumena,   *gearwost wisse,*   715

                     × × × / × /
fættum fahne.   Ne wæs þæt forma sið⌒   B

× / / \ ×
þæt he Hroþgares   ham gesohte;

næfre he on aldordagum   ær ne siþðan

                    / \ × /
heardran hæle,   healðegnas fand.   E

[6] See pp. 99–100 above.

> *Com þa to recede*   rinc siðian,   720
>
> *dreamum bedæled.*   Duru sona onarn,
>
>   ×   × × × × ／ ×   × ／
> fyrbendum fæst,   syþðan he hire folmum æthran.   B
>   710–22

In each case the end-stopping, together with the stress pattern, draws attention to a key point: to Grendel's enmity with God; to the site of his intended crime; to the men against whom his malice is directed, and finally to the touch of his hand which was sufficient to open the iron-bound door. The effect depends on the combinations of half-lines rather than on the individual half-lines. The pause at the end of lines 711 and 713 arises partly because in each case the following line begins with a strongly-stressed syllable; in lines 716–17, by contrast, the lightly-stressed *þæt* allows the two lines to function as a single rhythmic unit and the emphasis on the phrase *forma sið* comes from the unstressed syllables which precede it. This kind of effect is not confined to the major breaks, marked in modern editions by full-stops and semi-colons. In the following passage the unstressed syllables at the beginning of lines 704a and 707b tend to create a pause and therefore an emphasis on the words *hornreced* and *sceadu* just as in line 705b they create a pause between sense-groups. The effect is particularly noticeable in line 707 where the first stress of the D-type half-line is omitted, creating a pause at the beginning of the line as well:

>   Com on wanre niht
>
> scriðan sceadugenga.   *Sceotend swæfon,*
>
>   ×   ×   ／ ＼ ×
> # þa þæt hornreced   *healdan scoldon,*
>
>   ×   ×   ／ ×   ／
> *ealle buton anum.* # Þæt wæs yldum cuþ   B   705
>
> þæt hie ne moste,   þa metod nolde,
>
>   × ／ ＼ ×   ×   ×   ⌣   ／ ×
> # se scynscaþa # under sceadu bregdan;   C
>
> ac he wæccende   *wraþum on andan*
>
> bad bolgenmod   *beadwa geþinges.*
>   702–9

A further point of interest in this passage is the treatment of the repeats of the verb *com*. In line 702b the stress does not fall on the verb but on the words which describe the manner of Grendel's coming,

     × × ╱ × ╱
com on wanre niht   702b

similarly in line 710 the emphasis is on the time and place,

   ╱ × × ╱ ×
ða com of more   710

but the third time the word is used it carries the stress, and the metre enhances the syntactic climax,

   ╱ × × ╲ ×
com þa to recede.   720

In the next few lines the rhythm changes very noticeably. The number of A-type half-lines drops sharply, so that the underlying rhythm is obscured, and the common D + A and A + B combinations are replaced by combinations of E, B and D-type half-lines:

Com þa to recede	rinc siðian,	D	720
dreamum bedæled.	Duru sona onarn,	E	
E *fyrbendum fæst,*	syþðan he hire folmum æthran;	B	
D *onbræd þa bealohydig,*	ða he gebolgen wæs,	B	
recedes mu þan.	Raþe æfter þon	E	
B *on fagne flor*	feond treddode,	D	725
D *eode yrremod;*	him of eagum stod	B	
ligge gelicost	leoht unfæger.	D	
			720–27

The effect of this concentration of lines with secondary stresses and with heavy end stress, together with the unbalanced effect created by the asymmetrical D and E-types, is to hold up the forward progress of the verse: the normal even rhythm is replaced by an irregular distribution of stresses, an effect enhanced by the lines with a large number of lightly-stressed syllables (722–3). A similar effect is created, though on a smaller scale, in the description of Grendel devouring Hondscio, a passage which is marked by a series of abrupt rhythmical shifts:

Þ́ryðswýð behéold   E

D   mǽg Hígeláces,   hú sé manscáða

under fǽrgrípum   geféran wolde.   C

Né þæt se aglǽca   *yldan þohte,*

C   ac hé geféng hráðe   *forman siðe*   740

E   slǽpendne rínc,   slát unwearnúm,   D

D   bát bánlocan,   blód édrum dranc,   D

E   synsnǽdum swealh;   *sona hǽfde*

D   unlýfigendes   *eal gefeormod,*

fet ond folma.   Forð néar ǽtstop,   E   745

nam þa mid handa   hígeþihtigne   D

rinc on ræste,   rǽhte ongéan   E

feond mid folme;   hé onféng hráþe   C

inwitþancum   ónd wíð earm gesǽt.   B

                                                     736-49

The irregular rhythm of this passage is stabilized briefly at line 738 by
a return to a rhythm based on A and C-types, only to break down
again in the actual description of the monster swallowing the corpse
(741-3); the normal rhythm is resumed at the words *sona hæfde.*

   The last line of this passage illustrates a feature which occurs
repeatedly in the descriptions of the monster fights: the use of an
emphatic cadence to distinguish the main points in the action. The B-
type half-line *ond wið earm gesæt* (749b) marks Beowulf's first move in
the contest; up to this point, all the action has come from Grendel.
Beowulf's second move comes when, having maintained his grip on
the monster's arm, he stands up to grapple with him (760a); again the
point is made with a B-type cadence:

   Gemunde þa se goda,   mæg Higelaces,   D

   æfenspræce, uplang astod   E

B   ond hím fǽstè wiðfèng.

758–60

The culmination of the fight, when Beowulf lays down the hand, is indicated in the same emphatic way:

syþðan hildedeor   *hond alegde,*

earm ond eaxle   (þær wæs eal geador   C

Grendles grape)   under geápnè hróf.   B

834–6

These are not of course the only B-type cadences in the description of the fight (736–836): others occur at lines 756a, 766b, 797b and 821a, all points worthy of emphasis. It is notable however that both here and in the description of the fight with Grendel's mother, the crucial points in the action are never associated with the more usual lightly-stressed cadences. The failure of the sword borrowed from Unferth (1528b), the throwing of Grendel's mother to the floor (1540b), Beowulf's fall (1544b), his recovery of his footing (1556b), the death of his adversary (1568b) and his decapitation of the dead Grendel (1590b) are all associated with B-type cadences. Elsewhere in the account of the second fight the symmetrical and asymmetrical rhythms found earlier in association with speeches and descriptions of violent action appear again in similar contexts. After Unferth's sword fails, Beowulf, remembering his reputation, throws the blade to the ground and decides to rely on his strength. The poet interposes a general comment on the behaviour proper to a hero and, as in Beowulf's own formal boasts, establishes the matter in a series of C-type half-lines:

strenge getruwode,

mundgripe mægenes.   Swá scéal man dón,   C

þonne he æt guðe   gégan þénceð   C

E   longsumne lof,   ná ymb his líf cearáð.   C

1533–6

Again, when Beowulf cuts off Grendel's mother's head with the magic sword the A-type rhythms give way to the more irregular D and E-type patterns:

	He gefeng þa fetelhilt,	freca Scyldinga	D
	hreoh ond heorogrim	hringmæl gebrægd,	E
D	aldres orwena,	yrringa sloh,	E 1565
	þæt hire wið halse	heard grapode,	D
E	banhringas bræc.	Bil eal ðurhwod	E
D	fægne flæschoman;	heo on flet gecrong.	B
	Sweord wæs swatig,	secg weorce gefeh.	D

1563–9

Old English poetry is a spoken art and one might therefore expect that the speeches of characters in the poems would reveal an awareness of colloquial rhythms. A study of the speeches in *Beowulf* suggests that different rhythmic elements were associated with different levels of formality. Beowulf's opening address to the coastguard which is remarkable for its careful circumlocutions, has an equally striking rhythm: in contrast to his more formal speeches, which contain large numbers of C-type half-lines, this speech begins with a series of half-lines which appear to have only one strong stress:

	Wē synt gumcynnes	*Geata leode*	260
	ond Higelaces	*heorðgeneatas.*	
	Wæs min fæder	*folcum gecyþed,*	
D	æþele ordfruma,	*Ecgþeow haten.*	
B	Gebad wintra worn,	ær he on weg hwurfe,	C
	gamol of geardum;	hine gearwe geman	B 265
	witena welhwylc	*wide geond eorþan.*	

260–66

The question of how to scan these lines involves a number of rather abstract problems. The normal rhythm of Old English verse requires two strongly-stressed elements in each half-line. When, therefore, a half-line appears to have only one such element there must be some factor which compensates for the apparently missing stress. Bliss suggests that a series of lightly-stressed syllables can be equivalent to a strongly-stressed one, and Cable argues that half-lines like *ond Higelaces* which Bliss identifies as a D-type without the first strong stress should be considered as light-weight C-type half-lines, the secondary stress counting as though it were a strong stress.[7] What is important here however is not abstract theory but performance. The fact that these lines occur in such large numbers implies that they were metrically acceptable, yet there is still a difference to the ear between a half-line like,

$$\overset{\times}{\text{þa}}\ \overset{\times}{\text{þæt}}\ \overset{/}{\text{horn}}\overset{\backslash\ \times}{\text{reced}}\qquad\qquad\qquad 704a$$

where the two stresses fall within one word and lines like,

$$\overset{\times}{\text{on}}\ \overset{/}{\text{land}}\ \overset{/\ \times}{\text{Dena}}\qquad\qquad\qquad 253b$$

where they belong to two different words. Moreover the same form can appear in quite different metrical contexts. The genitive of *Hygelac*, for instance, appears in line 2386b as the second part of a D-type half-line:

$$\overset{/}{\text{sunu}}\ \overset{/}{\text{Hy}}\text{ge}\overset{\backslash\ \times}{\text{laces}}\qquad\qquad\qquad 2386b$$

It seems logical to believe that it conforms to the same stress-pattern when it occurs in the half-line *ond Higelaces*, and that this second half-line, though metrically acceptable, is really a light-weight D-type. If one accepts this distinction between metrical theory and performance and then considers the rhythm of these lines in relation to their content and context it is possible to see some correlation.

In general, the speeches in *Beowulf* contain a higher proportion of light half-lines than the narrative sections of the poem; light lines form about 14 per cent of the opening narrative (1–236) and about 22 per cent of the speeches in the first five hundred lines. There are, moreover, differences between the speeches. First there is a distinction based on rank and familiarity.[8] When Beowulf arrives in Denmark he is challenged by the coastguard and later by Wulfgar before he is allowed to enter Hrothgar's hall. Beowulf's speeches to these two officials (260–85, 342–7) both begin with a light half-line; they, on the other hand, begin their speeches to Beowulf with a normal half-line (237–57, 287–300, 316–19, 333–9, 350–55). When Wulfgar addresses

---

[7] Bliss, *Metre of Beowulf*, pp. 6–23 and 108; Cable, *Meter and melody*, pp. 20–31 and pp. 65–74 (clashing stress). See also T. Cable, 'Rules for syntax and metrics in *Beowulf*', pp. 81–8.

[8] Compare the distinction between *tu* and *vous* in French, or between *thou* and *you* in Middle English.

Hrothgar however (361–70) he begins his speech with a light half-line and when he returns to welcome the visitors inside the hall he addresses them in the same way (391–8). It seems likely that two factors are involved here. First there is a difference in rank between Beowulf and these officials which requires that they should address him formally while he is free to speak more casually. Secondly, there is an element of familiarity. Wulfgar and Hrothgar have a relationship based on friendship as well as allegiance: Hrothgar is the *winedryhten* (360) and it is therefore appropriate that Wulfgar should speak to him and to the newcomer, Beowulf, in different ways. His change of tone when he returns to Beowulf, who has been waiting outside the hall, is the result of Hrothgar's explanation that Beowulf is not a stranger but the son of an old friend, and someone whom he had known as a boy.

The relationship between Beowulf and Hrothgar is likewise indicated by a change of rhythm. Beowulf's speech when he first enters Heorot is formal and ceremonious, and the rhythm of his opening greeting is equally formal:

B   Wæs þu, Hroðgar, hal!   Ic eom Higelaces

    mæg ond magoðegn;   hæbbe ic mærða fela   B

    ongunnen on geogoþe.

    407–9

Hrothgar replies in the same manner:

B   For gewyrhtum þu,   *wine min Beowulf*

    ond for arstafum   *usic sohtest.*

    457–8

It is notable however that in both speeches the formal words of address are followed immediately by a light half-line, as if to retreat from formality into a more conversational tone. Hrothgar's speech in particular has a large number of these light lines:

B   Gesloh þin fæder   *fæhðe mæste*;

    wearþ he Heaþolafe   to handbonan   460

    mid Wilfingum;   ða hine Wedera cyn   B

    for herebrogan   *habban ne mihte.*

$\times \times \times \times / \times$
Þanon he gesohte   Suðdena folc   E

B   ofer yða gewealc,   Arscyldinga.   D

459–64

A similar effect is found in Hygelac's speech welcoming Beowulf home, where the two sentences which begin with light half-lines (1990b, 1992b) create an impression of spontaneous speech:

Hu lomp eow on lade,   *leofa Biowulf,*

$\times \quad \times \quad / \quad \backslash \times$
þa ðu færinga   *feorr gehogodest*

sæcce secean   ofer sealt wæter,   C

                      $\times \quad \times \quad / \quad \backslash \times$
hilde to Hiorote?   Ac ðu Hroðgare   1990

E   widcuðne wean   *wihte gebettest,*

             $\times \quad \times \quad / \quad \backslash \times$
mærum ðeodne?   Ic ðæs modceare

E   sorhwylmum seað,   *siðe ne truwode*

leofes mannes;   ic ðe lange bæd   B

$\times \quad \times \quad \times \times / \quad \backslash$
þæt ðu þone wælgæst   *wihte ne grette,*   1995

D   lete Suðdene   *sylfe geweorðan*

guðe wið Grendel.   *Gode ic þanc secge*

$\times \quad \times . \quad \times \quad \times / \quad \times$
þæs ðe ic ðe gesundne   geseon moste.   C

1987–98

This informality typifies so many of the speeches that when it does not occur one tends to ask why. Light half-lines are rare in Wealhtheow's speeches, perhaps because both are connected with the ceremonies of the hall, the cup-giving (1169–87) and the presentation of the neck-lace (1216–31). Beowulf on the other hand hardly ever begins his speeches in a formal way: the only examples in the first two parts of the poem are his greeting to Hrothgar (407–55), the speech encourag-ing Hrothgar after the death of Æschere (1384–96), the solemn speech he makes before entering the lake, reminding the old king of the promise he had made to be a father to him (1474–91), and the reply to Unferth (530–606). In the last part of the poem, the dragon fight, the tone of the speeches changes as if to harmonize with the sadness and foreboding which colour the final sections of the poem. Beowulf's two speeches immediately before the fight both begin with a full half-line (2511b, 2518b) as does his speech after the fight, when he thinks sadly of his lack of an heir (2729–51). In his two later speeches however, as he gazes on the dragon's gold (2794–2808) and says farewell to Wiglaf, the last of his family (2813–16), he reverts to a more conversational tone. Wiglaf himself, whether speaking to his friends, to Beowulf or about him, uses this colloquial rhythm only once (2864–91), when he reviles Beowulf's cowardly retainers:

Þæt, la, mæg secgan   se ðe wyle soð specan   C

þæt se mondryhten   se eow ða maðmas geaf,   B   2865

eoredgeatwe,   þe ge þær on standað,   C

þonne he on ealubence   *oft gesealde*

D   healsittendum   *helm ond byrnan,*

þeoden his þegnum,   swylce he þrydlicost

B   ower feor oððe neah   *findan meahte,*   2870

þæt he genunga   *guðgewædu*

wraðe forwurpe,   ða hyne wig beget.   B
2864–72

The opening phrase is identical with that used by Hrothgar to Beowulf (1700) but in this different context the familiar tone conveys a contempt analogous to that implied by Unferth in his attack on Beowulf:

Eart þu se Beowulf,   se þe wið Brecan wunne.   506

These changes in tone are connected with the relationships between characters, with the 'style of discourse';[9] they arise from the context rather than from the characters themselves. There is in fact little attempt to distinguish between characters by assigning a distinctive rhythm to them just as there is no attempt to provide individual characterization in other ways. Beowulf himself is shown simply as a hero in different situations. We are told a good deal about his

[9] For a definition of this term see M. A. K. Halliday, A. McIntosh and P. Strevens, *The linguistic sciences and language teaching*, pp. 92–3.

thoughts as well as his actions, we see into his mind, but we see him always as the hero, not as one particular and distinctive hero. The same is true of the other characters in the poem: they are noble, aristocratic, wise or brave according to their role in the poem, but they are not individualized. In rhythmic terms this can be seen from a comparison of the speeches of Unferth and Beowulf near the beginning of the poem (506–28, 530–606). Both speeches are distinctive in one respect: the proportions of A and D-type half-lines are lower than expected and those of the B, C and E-types are higher. The difference is greater in Unferth's speech than in Beowulf's, but it is a difference in degree rather than in kind. There is however one distinctive difference between the two: the cadences in Unferth's speech are A-type ones with the one exception of line 518,

$$\overset{\times\ \ \times\ \ /\times\ \ \ \diagup}{\text{hæfde mare mægen}}$$

where Unferth concludes his comparison between Beowulf and Breca with an emphatic evaluation of their comparative strength. Beowulf on the other hand ends a sentence with a B-type cadence five times, and this contributes to his more emphatic delivery: the cases are *ðonne ænig oðer man* (534), *ond þæt geæfndon swa* (538), *þurh mine hand* (558), *swa hit gedefe wæs* (561) ans *þonne his ellen deah* (573). With the exception of the general statement (573), all are telling points in the argument.

The openings of these two speeches have a wider interest. Unferth begins:

$$\overset{\times\ \ \ \times\ \ \times\ \ \ /}{\text{Eart þu se Beowulf,}}\qquad\text{se þe wið Brecan wunne,}\qquad\text{C}$$

B   on sidne sæ   ymb sund flite.   C

506–7

The rhythm of the passage as a whole, together with its content, suggests deliberate insolence, and a colloquial, unstressed opening would therefore be appropriate. Beowulf replies with a formality which is in striking contrast to the content of his speech:

$$\text{C}\qquad\text{Hwæt!}\qquad\overset{\times\ \ \ /\ \ \ \ /}{\text{þu worn fela,}}\qquad\textit{wine min Unferð,}$$

    beore druncen   ymb Brecan spræce,   C

    sægdest from his siðe.

530–32

The word *hwæt* is a call for attention, and one may imagine that a certain amount of noise followed Unferth's insults to the guest; a similar situation can be visualized when Beowulf returns in triumph with Grendel's head and addresses Hrothgar with the words:

Hwæt! we þe þas sælac sunu Healfdenes 1652

In the reply to Unferth however the word *hwæt* stood outside the normal metre, whereas this time it appears to form part of it, as it does in line 1774.[10] The status of the word *hwæt* is of some importance since it affects the reading of the opening lines of the poem. If the word lies outside the metre, then the poem begins with a light half-line:

Hwæt! We Gardena in geardagum,

D þeodcyninga *þrym gefrunon,*

hu ða æþelingas *ellen fremedon.*

1–3

The situations are similar, for the poet had to call for silence at the beginning of his recitation just as Beowulf had to call for silence at the beginning of his speech. If it was usual to begin a speech in conversational rhythm it is possible that the same was true of a poem, particularly one in which oral authority was emphasized. The problem is not confined to *Beowulf*, for *Andreas* and *Juliana* have similar first lines:

Hwæt! We gefrunan on fyrndagum

Andreas 1

Hwæt! We ðæt hyrdon hæleð eahtian

Juliana 1

Against these examples should be set four poems where the introductory *hwæt* clearly stands outside the line:

Hwæt! Ic swefna cyst secgan wylle

Dream of the rood 1

Hwæt! We feor and neah gefrigen habað

Exodus 1

Hwæt, me frod wita on fyrndagum

Vainglory 1

---

[10] Hwæt, me þæs on eþle edwenden cwom.

Hwæt! Ic ana sæt   innan bearwe

Judgment day II 1

If the word is to be treated consistently, it should always stand outside the verse, and in this case the opening lines of *Beowulf, Andreas, Juliana, Solomon and Saturn* and possibly also *The fates of the apostles* must be light. Other poems which seem to begin with a light half-line are *Christ and Satan, Christ III, The phoenix, The seafarer, Bede's death song* and *Elene*.[11] In some cases the lighter rhythm is associated with a poet-audience relationship based on a claim to shared experience, that is, a relationship of friendship rather than of authority; poems such as *Exodus* and *Genesis*, which derive from book-learning, begin with normal half-lines.[12] In other cases there seems to be a distinction between poems which are presented in a personal way and those which are more objective: *The seafarer*, which claims to be a true story, begins with a light half-line whereas *The wanderer* begins with a normal half-line. Elsewhere there may be a question of individual poetic preference: Cynewulf begins all four of his signed poems with lines which could be considered to be light:

Nu ðu geornlice   gæstgerynum

Christ II 1

Hwæt! We ðæt hyrdon   hæleð eahtian

Juliana 1

Þa wæs agangen   geara hwyrftum

Elene 1

Hwæt! Ic þysne sang   siðgeomor fand

Fates of the apostles 1

A question of some interest is whether the rhythmical devices found in *Beowulf* appear uniformly throughout the poetry in such contexts or whether they are typical of this particular poet. The speeches in Cynewulf's *Juliana*, like those in parts of *Beowulf*, contain many light half-lines. The following speech by Juliana's father illustrates this conversational tone:

[11] *Christ and Satan:* Þæt wearð underne   eorðbuendum
  Christ III: Ðonne mid fere   foldbuende
  Phoenix: Hæbbe ic gefrugnen   þætte is feor heonan
  Seafarer: Mæg ic be me sylfum   soðgied wrecan
  Bede's death song: Fore ðaem nedfere   nenig wiorðeð
  Elene: Þa wæs agangen   geara hwyrftum
[12] cf Chapter 3, pp. 36–7.

B   Ðu eart dohtor min   seo dyreste

ond seo sweteste   in sefan minum,   C

ange for eorþan,   minra eagna leoht,   B   95

Iuliana!   Þu on geaþe hafast

þurh þin orlegu   *unbiþyrfe*

B   ofer witena dom   *wisan gefongen.*

Juliana 93–8

Juliana herself, especially in her more aggressive and decisive
moments, seems to use fewer of these light lines:

Næfre ic þæs þeodnes   *þafian wille*

D   mægrædenne,   nemne he mægna god   B

geornor bigonge   þonne he gen dyde,   C   110

lufige mid lacum   þone þe leoht gescop,   B

heofon ond eorðan   ond holma bigong,   B

eodera ymbhwyrft.   Ne mæg he elles mec   B

bringan to bolde.   He þa brydlufan

sceal to oþerre   *æhtgestealdum*   115

idese secan;   nafað he ænige her.   B

Juliana 108–16

In Cynewulf's poetry however the light lines are not confined to the
speeches but are frequent in the poems as a whole, and it is possible
that he intended his writings to have a more conversational tone than
did epic poetry, even though he presents his heroines, Juliana and
Elene, in the manner and vocabulary of heroic verse. If this is so it
would be a matter of considerable critical importance. It was suggested earlier that distance from prose, in terms of rhythm, syntax
and vocabulary, was a mark of the high style associated with lofty

subjects.[13] The distinctive feature of Christian writings, as enunciated by Augustine, was that everything was lofty: there was no distinction or classification of themes. On the other hand, these themes were to be expressed in a simple style rather than a lofty one. Cynewulf's style is very much closer to that of prose than of verse, particularly in *Juliana*, and this may be an indication not, as is sometimes suggested, of late date, but of informality, the *sermo humilis* of Augustine transferred into Old English. Certainly *The battle of Maldon* which is considerably later has a much tighter rhythm.

Whereas the *Beowulf* poet tended to vary his rhythm within fairly strict limits, Cynewulf, starting with a looser rhythm more akin to that of prose, employs a wider variety of metrical devices. A passage which shows his technique well is the description of the battle of Constantine against the Huns near the beginning of *Elene* (105–37). This passage is a set-piece in a well-established tradition of battle poetry. As befits a formal piece of writing, the rhythm is not as free as it is in parts of *Juliana*, but it is well varied, to show the conventional items to advantage. The first part of the passage describes the preliminaries, with the inevitable reference to the beasts of battle:

	Heht þa on uhtan	*mid ærdæge*	105
	wigend wreccan,	*ond wæpenþræce*	
D	*hebban heorucumbul,*	*ond þæt halige treo*	B
C	*him beforan ferian*	*on feonda gemang,*	B
D	*beran beacen godes.*	*Byman sungon*	
	hlude for hergum.	*Hrefn weorces gefeah,*	D 110
	urigfeðra,	*earn sið beheold,*	D
E	*wælhreowra wig.*	*Wulf sang ahof,*	D
	holtes gehleða.	*Hildegesa stod.*	E

Elene 105–13

The first thing one notices is the small number of A-type half-lines. The second is the combination (105–106) of two normal half-lines with two light half-lines something which forces a pause before the words *mid ærdæge* and *ond wæpenþræce* and creates an emphasis on these

[13] See Chapter 2, pp. 16–17, and n. 11.

phrases. The next two lines show rhythmic combinations which are comparatively rare in *Beowulf*; moreover the use of a B-type rhythm in the second half of the line throws the emphasis on the final syllable, and draws attention to the fact that it was no ordinary banner that was carried into the enemy ranks but the standard of the cross. In the next two half-lines (109–10) the poet reestablishes the underlying A-type metre in his reference to the trumpets, before making his formal and conventional reference to the beasts of battle. This theme is expressed in a rhythm which emphasizes its patterned nature. Each of the three beasts, raven, eagle and wolf, is mentioned in two half-lines; in each case, the rhythm of the first half-line is the same, while in the second half-line it is varied. Where the rhythm is the same the syntax is the same; where the rhythm varies so too does the syntax. By this patterning the poet implies a resemblance between the three beasts, and creates the expectation of a fourth repeat in line 113. This expectation however is denied and the final statement, which gathers together the effects of these portents and preliminaries, while keeping a similar rhythm to that of the D-type half-lines, puts the matter more forcefully, with a strong final stress.

The patterned nature of these lines can be seen very clearly if one compares them with two other quite different treatments of the theme of the beasts of battle, those in *Judith* and in *Exodus*. In these two poems the battle and its accompaniments form an integral part of the narrative, not a mere preliminary as in *Elene*, and the description of the anticipatory beasts is a necessary part of that description. In *Elene*, on the other hand, Constantine's victory is simply a prerequisite for the story of his conversion and search for the true cross. The elaboration in the two heroic poems differs in kind: in *Judith* there is a greater concentration on the appearance and nature of the beasts, the dark coats and horny beaks of the birds and the expectancy of the lean wolf:

Þæs se hlanca gefeah		205
wulf in walde,	ond se wanna hrefn,	
wælgifre fugel.	Wiston begen	
þæt him ða þeodguman	þohton tilian	
fylle on fægum;	ac him fleah on last	
earn ætes georn,	urigfeðera,	210
salowigpada	sang hildeleoð,	
hyrnednebba.		

Judith 205–12

At that the lean wolf rejoiced in the wood, and the black raven, a bird greedy for carrion: both knew that the warriors intended to provide a feast from the doomed men; behind them flew the eagle, greedy for food, dewy-feathered, dark-coated, horny-beaked, and sang a battle-song.

In *Exodus* it is the power over the corpses which is stressed, for the beasts are choosers of the slain, and the wolves cheerful at the prospect of death; they form a parallel to the savage pursuers and intimate what the attitude of the Egyptians will be if they succeed in overcoming the Israelites; the similarity is enhanced by the use of the phrase *hare heorowulfas* (181) for the Egyptian troops, which, though conventional, is coloured by the earlier reference to the actual wolves:

> Hreopon herefugolas, hilde grædige,
> deawigfeðere ofer drihtneum,
> wonn wælceasega. Wulfas sungon
> atol æfenleoð ætes on wenan, 165
> carleasan deor, cwyldrof beodan
> on laðra last leodmægnes fyl.
>
> *Exodus* 162–7

The war-birds, greedy for battle, dewy-feathered, dark choosers of the dead, screamed above the corpses. The wolves sang a terrible evensong, hopeful of food, the uncaring beasts, longing for the slaughter, awaited from behind the enemy the death of the fighting-men.

Nothing distinguishes these two passages rhythmically from those surrounding them. Cynewulf, by contrast, writing a religious and theological treatise, chose to treat his battle scene in a style and manner different from that of the body of the poem, and made his set pieces ostentatiously formal as though to emphasize their allusive nature.

The account of the start to the fighting, has a similar ritualistic effect:

> B   Þær wæs borda gebrec   ond beorna geþrec,   B
>
> D   heard handgeswing   ond herga gring,   B
>
>   syððan heo earhfære   ærest metton.
>
> *Elene* 114–16

These lines have some of the formulaic quality of a passage from *The battle of Maldon*:

> B   Ða wearð borda gebræc.   *Brimmen wodon,*

guðe gegremode;   gár oft þurhwód   D

fæges feorhhus.

Battle of Maldon 295–7

The themes are similar but the technique of the passage from *Elene*, with its internal rhyme in lines 114 and 115 and its repeated syntactic and rhythmic patterns, is very different from that of the lines from *The battle of Maldon*. The same device of parallel syntax and parallel rhythm is used in the description of the attack by Constantine's army with reiterative effect; the sudden change of rhythm in line 123b produces a stand-still which corresponds to the climax and end to the action:

D   Stopon stiðhidige,   *stundum wræcon,*

D   bræcon bordhreðan,   bil in dufan,   D

D   þrungon þræchearde.   Þa wæs þuf hafen,   C   123

        segn for sweotum,   sigeleoð galen.

Elene 121–4

Finally, the flight of the Huns and the ways in which they evaded death are described in a series of lines constantly broken by light rhythms:

Súmé wig fórnam.   B

Súmé unsófte   *aldor generedon*

on þam héresíðe.   Súmé héalfcwice

flugon on fæsten   ond feore burgon

æfter stanclifum,   stede weardedon   D   135

ymb Dánubie.   Súmé drenc fórnam   B

on lágostreame   *lifes æt ende.*

Elene 131–7

In these lines rhythm is perfectly adapted to meaning. Of the four groups of people described, two die and two survive. Each group is referred to by the word *sume*; those who die do so in a B-type half-line; those who survive do so in a light half-line.

The places of death or of retreat are expressed in a series of light half-lines, and the whole passage resolves into metrical normality and physical finality in the half-line, *lifes æt ende*, one of the few with A-type rhythm.

In *Elene* Cynewulf chooses his rhythmic patterns to indicate a kind of quotation: traditional set pieces are expressed in a patterned series of rhythms which contrasts with his looser narrative style. He also uses rhythmic devices as a decorative, rhetorical feature. The easy narrative of *Christ II*, for instance, is interrupted by an elaborate rhyming passage in which the poet explains the implications of Christ's ascension:

Hwæt, we nu gehyrdan   hu þæt hælubearn

þurh his hydercyme   hals eft forgeaf,   E

gefreode ond gefreopade   folc under wolcnum,

D   mære meotudes sunu,   þæt nu monna gehwylc   B

cwic þenden her wunað,   geceosan mot   B   590

swa helle hienþu   swa heofones mærþu,

B   swa þæt leohte leoht   swa ða laþan niht,   B

swa þrymmes þræce   swa þystra wræce,

B   swa mid dryhten dream   swa mid deoflum hream,B

swa wite mid wraþum   swa wuldor mid arum,   595

B   swa lif swa deað,   swa hím leofre bið   B

to gefremmanne,   þenden flæsc ond gæst   B

wuniað in worulde.   Wuldor þæs age

E   þrynysse þrym,   *þonc butan ende!*

Christ 586–99

The contrasting choices (591–5) are expressed in a series of half-lines with parallel syntax, parallel rhythm and internal rhyme. Rhythm and syntax are closely interrelated.[14] Pairs of A-type half-lines alternate with pairs of B-type and this corresponds to the syntactic pattern so that phrases containing a genitive fill the A-type rhythm and phrases containing an adjective fill the B-type. This syntactic variation is further elaborated with the inversion of the phrase structure in lines 594–5 (*mid dryhten dream* → *wite mid wraþum*). The alternation of A and B-type rhythms is preserved in line 596 but the syntactic parallel is broken: the two alternatives, *swa lif swa deað*, are compressed into the first half-line and the *swa* of the second half-line, which is superficially similar to those in the preceding five lines, leads into a new syntax and a new idea:

$$\overset{\times}{swa} \overset{\times}{him} \overset{/}{leo} \overset{\times}{fre} \overset{/}{bi}ð$$

$$\overset{\times}{to} \overset{\times}{ge} \overset{/}{fremman} \overset{\times}{ne}$$

The change in thought is accompanied by a change in rhythm, with a light half-line replacing the expected A-type and without the endstopping of the earlier lines. Finally, as in the account of the battle in *Elene* (137), the passage is resolved by a return to the A-type rhythm, the conventional metre corresponding to the conventional phraseology:

> *wuldor þæs age*

> þrynysse þrym,   *þonc butan ende.*

Christ 598–9

Analysis of the work of the *Beowulf* poet and of Cynewulf, the one writing within a well-tried heroic tradition, the other adapting that tradition for exegetical ends, suggests the existence not only of an elaborate poetic technique but of a system of rhetoric which was based on rhythm rather than on figures of words and ideas. This rhetoric involved different levels of style, each of which was appropriate to a particular kind of composition or to a particular social relationship, whether formal or familiar. Shifts from one style to another were indicated by shifts in rhythm which were sufficiently distinctive to act as markers for changes in genre or to distinguish the traditional or conventional from what was fresh. Rhythmic variation was used not only for imitative effects, as in *Beowulf*, but as a decorative device analogous to the figures of words of Middle English and renaissance writers. In short, the rhythm was an essential element in the total meaning of the poems.

[14] For a discussion of the syntax of this passage see P. Clemoes, *Rhythm and cosmic order*, pp. 11–13.

Epilogue

8 Private poetry

In this book Old English poetry has been discussed largely in its social aspects, with reference to the triple relationship of poet, poem and audience. There are however a few poems which, although public in the sense that they are preserved in anthologies and not in the author's manuscript, seem to have been intended for the use of private individuals rather than for public recitation or reading. Three of these poems will be discussed here: *A prayer, Resignation* and *The dream of the rood*. These poems are very different from the other verse prayers of the period: the communal meditations known as *Christ I*, and the paraphrases and expansions of the *Pater noster, Credo* and *Gloria*. In different ways all three illustrate the movement which took place in the late Anglo-Saxon period away from that kind of prayer which was concerned with universal needs, and towards the expression, often in emotional and contrived language, of the more intimate feelings of the individual..

The *Prayer* is addressed to God the judge and, like many prayers of the late Anglo-Saxon period, is an appeal for mercy at the hour of death.[1] The artistry shows itself largely in the form, for, with one exception, the ideas and the language are commonplace. The prayer falls into three parts: in the first (1–7) the poet calls on God, the best of doctors, to heal the soul which has been wounded by sin;[2] in the second (8–20) he contrasts the wretchedness of the man beset by sin with the happiness of the righteous; in the third (21–79) he praises God's nobility and power, contrasting his greatness with man's smallness and propensity to sin. The meaning is conveyed through a series of oppositions and this is reflected in the syntax, with its parallels and variations. The technique is similar to that of *The seafarer* 106–7:

---

[1] See the Latin prayers in Cotton Titus D. xxvii, ff. 66–70, and the vernacular prayers in Royal 2 B. v and Tiberius A. iii; the vernacular prayers are printed in H. Logeman, 'Anglo-Saxonica minora', *Anglia* 11 (1888), pp. 97–120 and *Anglia* 12 (1889), pp. 497–518.
[2] The metaphor of the doctor is found in the prayer *De latere domini* in the Book of Nunnaminster, Harley 2965, ff. 30–30ᵛ, printed in W. de Gray Birch, *An ancient manuscript of the eighth or ninth century*, Hampshire Record Society (1889), p. 77.

> Dol biþ se þe him his dryhten ne ondrædeþ;
> cymeð him se deað unþinged.
> Eadig bið se þe eaþmod leofaþ;   cymeð him seo ar of
> heofonum.

Foolish is the man who does not fear his lord; death will come to him unexpectedly. Blessed is the man who lives humbly; mercy will come to him from heaven.

⌈In *The seafarer* the syntactic figure serves to draw attention to the poet's conclusion: it is an isolated decorative item.[3] ⌉In the *Prayer* by contrast it provides a structure for the poem as a whole. Much of part two of the prayer consists of two sentences whose words and rhythm parallel each other exactly. The simple framework accentuates the few words which differ: *earming* contrasted with *eadig*, *deofol* set against *dryhten* and *mirigð* against *geweorc*:

I   *Se byð* earming   *þe on eorðan her*
      dæiges and nihtes   deofle campað
      and hys willan wyrcð;   wa *him* þære mirigðe,
      þonne he ða handlean   *hafað and sceawað*,
      bute he þæs yfeles   ær geswyce.   15
II   *Se byð* eadig,   se *þe on eorðan her*
      dæiges and nyhtes   drihtne hyræð
      and a hys willan wyrcð;   wel *hym* þæs geweorkes,
      ðonne he ða handlean   *hafað and sceawað*,
      gyf he ealteawne   ende gedreogeð.   20

Prayer 11–20

He is wretched who here on earth, day and night, fights against the devil and does his will; he will have woe in exchange for that joy, when he has and sees his reward, unless he first ceases from that evil. He is blessed who here on earth, day and night, serves God and always does his will; he will have good in exchange for that labour, when he has and sees his reward, if he makes a good end to his life.

In the third section of the prayer this patterned kind of writing is applied to an elaborate statement of God's greatness, which none in heaven or earth can tell. The ideas are similar to those found in St Paul's Prayer in the Epistle to the Ephesians (iii 14–21) and in Zophar's rebuke to Job (Job xi 7–9) but the expression of the ideas seems to be original to the poet. Like other writers, he evades the difficulty of describing the infinite by a rhetorical device: he claims

[3] cf *Beowulf* 183–8.

that what he wishes to say is inexpressible. Not only is God incomprehensible to men and to angels; his mystery is so great that he can hardly comprehend himself. The hyperbole develops from man, who cannot know the truth about an eternal God, through the angels, who are wiser than man but who, even so, cannot grasp the full extent of God's power, to God himself, the creator of man and ruler of the angels, whose understanding of himself is itself a mystery to man:

I   *Ne* mæg þe aherian   hæleða ænig;   30
    þeh us gesomnie   geond sidne grund,
    men ofer moldan,   geond ealne middaneard,
    ne mage we *næfre* asæcgan,   *ne þæt* soðe *witan,*
    hu þu æðele *eart,*   ece *drihten.*

II *Ne* þeah engla werod   up on heofenum   35
    snotra tosomne   sæcgan ongunnon,
    ne magon hy *næfre* areccean,   *ne þæt* gerim *wytan,*
    hu þu mære *eart,*   mihtig *drihten.*

III Ac is wunder mycel,   wealdend engla,
    gif þu hit sylfa wast,   sigores ealdor,   40
    hu þu mære *eart,*   mihtig and mægenstrang,
    ealra kyninga kyning,   Crist lifiende,
    ealra worulda scippend,   wealdend engla,
    ealra dugeþa duguð,   drihten hælend.

Prayer 30–44

Nor can any hero praise you; though he summon us men from across the broad deep, over the earth, from the whole world, we can never say or know the truth, how noble you are, eternal lord. Nor indeed can the armies of angels up in heaven, the company of wise ones, begin to say, nor can they ever reckon or compute how famous you are, mighty lord. But it is a great wonder, ruler of angels, lord of victory, if you yourself know how famous you are, mighty and strong, king of all kings, living Christ, creator of all worlds, lord of angels, glory of all glories, lord and saviour.

The lines describing the perplexity of men and of angels are constructed on the same pattern, for the difference between them is one of degree rather than of kind; the lines describing God's knowledge move from the apparent parallel of the sentence, *Ac is wunder mycel . . . gif þu hit sylfa wast . . . hu þu mære eart,* which suggests a third and higher level of mysteriousness, to a hymn of praise in which the bare statements appropriate to a perplexed creation are replaced by a series of titles through which finite man affirms those things which only God can understand. The poet then returns to his theme of

God's incomprehensibility, through a reference to the great paradox of his being, the incarnation:

Ðu eart se æðela   þe on ærdagum   45
ealra femnena wyn   fægere akende
on Bethleem ðære byrig   beornum to frofre,
eallum to are   ylda bearnum,
þam þe gelyfað   on lyfiendne god
and on þæt ece leoht   uppe on roderum.   50
Ðyn mægen ys swa mære,   mihtig drihten,

  I   swa *þæt ænig ne wat*   eorðbuende
þa deopnesse   drihtnes mihta,

  II   ne *þæt ænig ne wat*   engla hades
þa heahnisse   heofena kyninges.   55

Prayer 45–55

You are the noble one whom in days gone by the joy of all women graciously bore in the town of Bethlehem as a comfort to men, as a help to all the sons of men, for those who believe in the living God and in that eternal light up in the skies. Your power is so great, mighty lord, that none of those living on earth can know the depth of the lord's power, nor can any of angelic rank know the height of the king of heaven.

The main point in the argument is implied rather than stated: God's power was shown above all in the incarnation, when finite and infinite were united. Those on earth, to whom God descended, cannot comprehend the depth of his power; those in heaven, to whom he returned, cannot grasp its height.

In the *Prayer* the thought structure is conveyed in two ways: through the piling up of titles in the manner of encomiastic verse [4] and through syntactic repetition and variation. The poet of *Resignation* on the other hand voices his need for forgiveness through metaphor. The poem falls into five sections. In the first (1–9) the speaker commits himself, body and soul, to his creator; in the second (10–21) he asks God to show him the right way and asserts his intention to atone for his wickedness; in the third (22–40) he asks for time in which to repent; in the fourth (41–75) he prays for help at the hour of death and proclaims his readiness for the journey; finally (77–118) he talks of his poverty and exile, the endurance of which will bring him reward in heaven. The ideas are similar to those in the *Prayer* but the presentation is quite different. There is none of the syntactic patterning; instead, the poet draws on the imagery of other poems, setting his ideas within a scheme which is external to the poem itself. There is for

[4] See Chapter 2, p. 22 above.

instance the reference to man as part of the body of Christ (53), or the allusion to the devil as the thief who draws man into the darkness (15–16), which recalls both the darkness of evil and the judgment which will come like a thief in the night.[5] The clearest example however is the treatment of death as a voyage over the sea (70–76, 96–104). These lines recall parts of *The seafarer* but whereas in that poem the exile and the voyage are probably real, though with symbolic overtones, here they are clearly allegorical as they are in the epilogue to Cynewulf's *Christ* (850–68).[6] The poet looks forward with hope and adorns himself before setting out on the *ferðweg*, the path of the soul:

> Hwæþre ic me ealles þæs ellen wylle
> habban ond hlyhhan ond me hyhtan to,
> frætwian mec on ferðweg ond fundian
> sylf to þam siþe þe ic asettan sceal.
>
> *Resignation* 70–73

Nevertheless I will have courage in all that, and laugh and hope, adorn myself for the path of the soul and set out myself on that journey that I must make.

Later the poet describes himself as *fus on ferþe* (84) and *longunge fus* (98) phrases which are suggestive of death because of the constant association of the word *fus* with words like *fæge*.[7] The voyage for which the poet longs (97) is the voyage of death; when therefore he laments his lack of money for the journey (100–104) it should be taken in a symbolic way, as a reference to his lack of good deeds, the currency which will take him to heaven; the poverty is one of spirit. In such a case friends cannot help (102), for the journey of death is one which has to be made alone.

The third prayer, *The dream of the rood*, embodies ideas which are similar to those of *Resignation*, and shares some of its metaphors and vocabulary. It differs from it however because the main theme of the poem is conveyed through the over-all form of the poem. It is a dream-vision, a genre which became extremely popular later in the Middle Ages, and it claims to describe an actual vision enjoyed by the poet and to convey his reflections on it. But although the poem was

---

[5] cf *Beowulf* 707 and *Christ III* 867–74.
[6] D. Whitelock, 'The interpretation of *The seafarer*', in *The early cultures of north-west Europe*, ed. C. Fox and B. Dickins, pp. 259–72. On the imagery of *Resignation* see E. G. Stanley, 'Old English poetic diction', *Anglia* 73 (1955), pp. 413–66.
[7] *Beowulf* 1241, *fus ond fæge*. For *ferðweg* compare *The seafarer* 63, *wælweg*, G. V. Smithers, 'The meaning of *The seafarer* and *The wanderer*', *MÆ* 26 (1957), pp. 137–53, and 28 (1959), pp. 99–106. If the phrase in *Resignation* is emended to read *on forðweg* the reference is still to a journey of death, as in *The dream of the rood* 125 *afysed on forðwege* and *Guthlac* 801 *fusne on forðweg*.

composed with an eye to an audience, it draws on the traditions of meditative prayer. The poem is of interest, among other things, because it shows a close connection between form and content and this distinguishes it from the many other accounts of visions in the literature of the Anglo-Saxon period. Some of these visions, such as that of Cuthbert concerning Ecgfrith's defeat at Nechtanesmere or Edwin's vision concerning his return from exile to the Northumbrian throne, are prophetic; others, such as that of Dryhtelm, concern the last things, death, judgment, heaven and hell.[8] This second group is akin to the sermon *exemplum* in technique and purpose, designed to stir the listener to repentance before it was too late. *The dream of the rood* is reflective rather than exhortatory, and, unlike these other visions, it has a set and recognizable literary form.

The poem falls into four parts: a descriptive vision (4–23), a narrative vision (24–77), the address of the cross to the dreamer (78–121) and the dreamer's prayer (122–56). The whole is preceded by three introductory lines which identify the poem as a dream-vision. The form suggests that the poet was familiar with Macrobius's *Commentary on the Dream of Scipio*, a work which was known and used by Carolingian writers and which was widely read and quoted on the continent by the early tenth century. The book was available in England from the tenth century and Byrhtferth of Ramsey referred to it in his *Manual*.[9] Bede, too, used material from the *Commentary* though it is uncertain whether he knew it directly; the work was known in Ireland in the seventh and eighth centuries and he may have obtained his material from an Irish source.[10] *The dream of the rood* is the kind of dream known in Macrobius's classification as an *oraculum*, that is, a dream in which a revelation is made by some person of authority, in this case, the cross. This aspect of the genre is brought out in the closing passages where the cross asks the dreamer to relate this dream and to spread the message to others. The dream is also an example of the *somnium* or enigmatic dream which needs interpretation; the veiled allusions of the first, descriptive vision are interpreted in two

---

[8] *Bede's Ecclesiastical History*, ed. B. Colgrave and R. A. B. Mynors, Bk. II, ch. xii, pp. 176–81 and Bk. V, ch. xii, pp. 488–97; *Two lives of St Cuthbert*, ed. B. Colgrave, pp. 122–3.

[9] M. Schedler, *Die Philosophie des Macrobius und ihr Einfluss auf die Wissenschaft des Christlichen Mittelalters, Beitr. zur Geschichte der Philosophie des Mittelalters, Texte und Untersuchungen* Bd xiii, Heft 1 (1916), pp. 106–7; J. D. A. Ogilvy, *Books known to the English, 597–1066*, pp. 196–7; *Byrhtferth's Manual*, ed. S. J. Crawford, EETS 177 (1929), pp. 16–17, notes to lines 20, 28.

[10] C. W. Jones, *Bedae Opera de Temporibus*, pp. 340, 361; *Macrobius: Commentary on the Dream of Scipio*, transl. W. H. Stahl, pp. 42–7. Dreambooks, that is, collections of interpretations of dreams, are found in several tenth and eleventh-century English manuscripts, showing that there was an interest in the subject: *Leechdoms, wortcunning and starcraft of early England*, ed. O. Cockayne, Rolls Ser. 35 (1864–6), iii, pp. 169–77, 199–215; L. Thorndike, *A history of magic and experimental science*, II, pp. 294–5.

ways: by the second, narrative vision, and more explicitly by the cross's address to the dreamer.

The form of the poem not only provides an exceptionally tidy structure and framework for the thought; it is appropriate to a meditative poem in a more subtle way. At an early period religious writers took over a number of words which already had extensive connotations in classical literature and applied them to the subject of prayer.[11] Among the more important of these words were *quies, otium, vacatio* and *sabbatum*. All four resemble one another in drawing attention to the leisure necessary for prayer. *Quies* referred originally to a state of tranquillity, often associated with the tranquillity of sleep and contrasted with the state of wakefulness; in patristic writings sleep which refreshes the body became a symbol of the quietness of mind in which we await the coming of God. Sleep is not slothfulness but something fecund: while Adam slept in Paradise Eve was brought forth from his side; when Christ, the second Adam, slept on the cross, the Church was brought forth from his side. From here it is an easy step to the idea that sleep and death are related. Sleep of course is often used as a symbol for death,[12] but in Christian writings the idea is reversed and death becomes merely a sleep: as Christ slept on the cross so the faithful sleep in Christ in a *quies aeterna*, the tranquillity of heaven. The peace of heaven was symbolized too by the word *sabbatum*. The Jewish sabbath commemorated the rest of God on the seventh day of creation; the Christian sabbath recalled the rest of Christ on the cross and in the tomb on the seventh day, and his resurrection on the first or eighth day. But whereas the Jewish sabbath was concerned solely with physical rest, the Christian sabbath involved rest or recreation for the soul, a rest which would be complete only in heaven. The Christian sabbath therefore looked forward to the end of the world: it prefigured and partially anticipated the eternal sabbath of heaven.[13] The two other words, *otium* and *vacatio*, are concerned with freedom from work. In classical times the word *otium* had a double meaning—idleness or leisure—but from the time of Augustine onwards it came to refer to the leisure which left one free to contemplate God. Finally, *vacatio* was used of the emptiness which left one open to God—at his disposal—and, in particular, the emptiness of the sabbath holiday. All four of these words have in common the idea that rest and meditation in this world are a foretaste of the eternal rest and contemplation of the next.

---

[11] The material on the vocabulary of prayer is drawn from the following two works: J. Leclercq, 'Études sur le vocabulaire monastique du moyen âge', *Studia Anselmiana* 48 (1961) and 'Études sur le vocabulaire de la contemplation au moyen âge', *Studia Anselmiana* 51 (1963).

[12] e.g. *Solomon and Saturn* 313, *slæp bið deaðe gelicost*.

[13] *Byrhtferth's Manual*, ed. S. J. Crawford, pp. 214–15.

These ideas are clearly present behind the words of *The dream of the rood* even though they are not fully explicit. The revelation which comes to the dreamer is concerned with devotion to the cross: just as Christ suffered and so entered into glory (Luke xxiv 26) so the cross, which participated in his sufferings, now shares his glory and man can do the same; by honouring the cross he shares in Christ's death and can attain the new life which came through Christ's death. The poem is therefore eschatological in intent, and this is clear from the opening vision where the jewelled and blood-stained cross attended by angels is the sign which will appear at the end of the world, while the wounds in the cross are related to Christ's showing of his wounds to mankind at the last judgment.[14] When the dreamer prays to the cross he does not look back to the death of Christ, which it commemorates, but forward to his own death and resurrection:

> Gebæd ic me þa to þan beame   bliðe mode,
> elne mycle,   þær ic ana wæs
> mæte werede.   Wæs modsefa
> afysed on forðwege,   feala ealra gebad   125
> langunghwila.   Is me nu lifes hyht
> þæt ic þone sigebeam   secan mote
> ana oftor   þonne ealle men,
> well weorþian.

Dream of the rood 122–9

Then I prayed to that tree with a joyful heart, with great power, where I was alone with few companions. My mind was ready to depart, I suffered many hours of longing. Now my hope of life rests in the fact that I can seek the tree of victory alone more often than other men, honour it well.

The joyful expectation is identical with that in the last part of the poem *Resignation*. The readiness for death, the longing for the next world and the hope with which both poets anticipate it are all essential parts of contemplation:

> Contemplatio est spei in hoc spatio per fidem, non repraesentatio, nec possessio, sed expectatio.[15]

---

[14] On the eschatological elements see J. V. Fleming, '*The dream of the rood* and Anglo-Saxon monasticism', *Traditio* 22 (1966), pp. 43–72; Barbara Raw, '*The dream of the rood* and its connections with early Christian art', *MÆ* 39 (1970), pp. 239–56.

[15] Tertullian, *De resurrectione*, xxiii 7, *Corpus Christianorum, Series Latina* II (1954), p. 950, quoted in Leclercq, *Studia Anselmiana* 48, p. 88. The key words are as follows:

The expression however is different in the two poems for in *The dream of the rood* the idea is integrated into the structure of the poem as a whole in order to express a theory of prayer.

In the opening lines of *The dream of the rood* the poet calls attention to three things: that he was dreaming, that the time was midnight and that the world was silent:

> Hwæt! Ic swefna cyst   secgan wylle,
> hwæt me gemætte   to midre nihte,
> syðþan reordberend   reste wunedon!
>
> *Dream of the rood* 1–3

Listen! I will relate the best of dreams which I dreamed in the middle of the night, after men with their voices were at rest.

By using the word *swefn* 'dream' the poet links himself with visionaries such as the poet Cædmon or the dreamers of the Old Testament, but more importantly, he associates himself with the contemplative ideal summed up in the phrase, 'Ego dormio sed cor meum vigilat' (Song of songs v 2). Sleep is a symbol of prayer; in turn, both sleep and prayer symbolize the repose of death and of the world to come. It is appropriate therefore that a poem concerned with death and resurrection should be cast in the form of a dream. That the time is midnight is also appropriate for this is, above all, the hour at which God manifests himself to man. The death of the first-born of the Egyptians, on the occasion of the first passover, took place at midnight (Exodus xi 4–5). The birth of Christ, the true paschal lamb, took place at midnight (Wisdom xviii 14–15), as would the second coming, at the consummation of the world (Matt. xxiv 42–4). The silence which surrounds the dreamer is the silence which is conducive to prayer but it is also the silence in which God shows himself as he did at his birth:

> Dum medium silentium tenerent omnia, et nox in suo cursu medium iter haberet, omnipotens sermo tuus, Domine, de caelis a regalibus sedibus venit.[16]

	Dream of the rood	*Resignation*			*Seafarer*
hyht and *hyhtan:*	126	71			45
longung:	126	98			46
fus and *afysed:*	125	84	88	98	50
forðweg, ferðweg, wælweg:	125	72			63
eþel:	156	89			cf 38
					elþeodigra eard

[16] Introit of the mass for the Sunday after Christmas, Wisdom xviii 14–15.

It is because God shows himself so suddenly and unexpectedly that man should keep watch and pray, especially at midnight, the hour at which God was expected to appear to man for the last time.[17]

These three poems although concerned with the intimate thoughts of their authors are far from being spontaneous outpourings of piety. On the contrary, all three show a careful and elaborate rhetoric. In the *Prayer* the elaboration is one of syntax, using repetitions of word patterns to indicate the shape of the thought; in *Resignation* the elaboration is one of metaphor by which the poet relates his own poverty of spirit and exile from his true home in heaven to the misery of solitaries and exiles like the wanderer and the seafarer; in *The dream of the rood* the shape of the poem itself becomes a symbol of its content, and sleep the image of death becomes the way of prayer which both prepares one for death and rebirth and prefigures those things to which it leads.

[17] *The Benedictine Office*, ed. J. M. Ure, pp. 81–2 and 100–101.

Bibliography

Abbreviations

ASE   *Anglo-Saxon England*
ASPR   *Anglo-Saxon poetic records*
CSEL   *Corpus scriptorum ecclesiasticorum latinorum*
EEMF   Early English Manuscripts in facsimile
EETS   Early English Text Society
JEGP   *Journal of English and Germanic Philology*
MÆ   *Medium Ævum*
MLN   *Modern Language Notes*
MP   *Modern Philology*
NM   *Neuphilologische Mitteilungen*
N & Q   *Notes and Queries*
PBA   *Proceedings of the British Academy*
RES   *Review of English Studies*
SP   *Studies in Philology*

1 Manuscripts

For descriptions of all manuscripts containing Old English see:
    N. Ker, *Catalogue of manuscripts containing Anglo-Saxon* (Oxford, 1957);
    'A supplement to *Catalogue of manuscripts containing Anglo-Saxon*', *ASE* 5 (1976), 121–31.
For illuminated manuscripts see:
    J. J. G. Alexander, *Insular manuscripts from the 6th to the 9th century* (London, forthcoming);
    E. Temple, *Anglo-Saxon manuscripts 900–1066* (London, 1976).
For facsimiles of the four main manuscripts see:
    The *Beowulf* manuscript, London British Library, Cotton Vitellius A. xv, ff. 94–209: *Beowulf, Autotypes with a transliteration and notes*, ed. J. Zupitza, EETS 77 (1882).
    The Exeter book, Exeter Cathedral 3501, ff. 8–130: *The Exeter book of Old English poetry*, ed. R. W. Chambers, M. Foerster and R. Flower (London, 1933).
    The Junius manuscript, Oxford, Bodleian Library, Junius 11: *The Caedmon manuscript of Anglo-Saxon biblical poetry*, ed. I. Gollancz (Oxford, 1927).
    The Vercelli book, Vercelli, Biblioteca Capitolare cxvii: *Il codice Vercellese con omelie e poesie in lingua anglosassone*, ed. M. Foerster (Rome, 1913).

The compilation of the manuscripts is discussed in the following works:

K. Sisam, *Studies in the history of Old English literature* (Oxford, 1953), Ch. 5 'The compilation of the *Beowulf* manuscript' and Ch. 6 'The Exeter book'.

D. G. Scragg, 'The compilation of the Vercelli book', *ASE* 2 (1973), 189–207.

Barbara Raw, 'The probable derivation of most of the illustrations in Junius 11 from an illustrated Old Saxon *Genesis*', *ASE* 5 (1976), 133–48.

See also the introductions to the editions listed under 2 below.

2 Editions

Complete edition:

The Anglo-Saxon poetic records, ed. G. P. Krapp and E. van K. Dobbie (New York, 1931–53), 6 vols.

Selected individual texts:

i Poetry

The advent lyrics of the Exeter book, ed. J. J. Campbell (Princeton, 1959).

Andreas and the fates of the apostles, ed. K. R. Brooks (Oxford, 1961).

The battle of Maldon, ed. E. V. Gordon (London, 1937).

Beowulf and the fight at Finnsburg, ed. F. Klaeber, 3rd edn. (Boston, 1936).

The manuscripts of Cædmon's hymn and Bede's death song, ed. E. van K. Dobbie (New York, 1937).

Christ and Satan, ed. M. D. Clubb (New Haven, 1925).

Daniel and Azarias, ed. R. T. Farrell (London, 1974).

Deor, ed. K. Malone (London, 1933).

The dream of the rood, ed. M. F. Swanton (Manchester, 1970).

Three Old English elegies: the Wife's lament, the Husband's message, the Ruin, ed. R. F. Leslie (Manchester, 1961).

Elene, ed. P. Gradon (London, 1958).

Exodus, ed. E. B. Irving (New Haven, 1953).

The later Genesis, ed. B. J. Timmer (Oxford, 1954).

Judith, ed. B. J. Timmer (London, 1961).

Juliana, ed. R. Woolf (London, 1955, corrected, 1966).

The phoenix, ed. N. F. Blake (Manchester, 1964).

The seafarer, ed. I. L. Gordon (London, 1960).

The poetical dialogues of Solomon and Saturn, ed. R. J. Menner (New York, 1941).

Waldere, ed. F. Norman (London, 1933).

The wanderer, ed. R. F. Leslie (Manchester, 1966); ed. T. P. Dunning and A. J. Bliss (London, 1969).

Widsith, ed. K. Malone (Copenhagen, 1962).

ii Prose

Ælfrics Grammatik und Glossar, ed. J. Zupitza (Berlin, 1880).
Homilies of Ælfric: a supplementary collection, ed. J. C. Pope, EETS 259–60 (1967–8).
King Alfred's Old English version of Boethius De consolatione philosophiae, ed. W. J. Sedgefield (Oxford, 1899).
Benedictine Office, ed. J. M. Ure (Edinburgh, 1957).
Byrhtferth's manual, ed. S. J. Crawford, EETS 177 (1929).
Two Saxon chronicles parallel, ed. J. Earle and C. Plummer (Oxford, 1892–99), 2 vols.
Ancient laws and institutes of England, ed. B. Thorpe (London, 1840), 2 vols.
Leechdoms, wortcunning and starcraft of early England, ed. O. Cockayne, Rolls Ser. 35 (1864–6).
The dialogue of Salomon and Saturnus, ed. J. M. Kemble (London, 1848).
The homilies of Wulfstan, ed. D. Bethurum (Oxford, 1957).

iii Latin texts

Monumenta Alcuiniana, ed. P. Jaffé (Berlin, 1873).
Asser's Life of King Alfred, ed. W. H. Stevenson, rev. D. Whitelock (Oxford, 1959).
Bede's Ecclesiastical history, ed. B. Colgrave and R. A. B. Mynors (Oxford, 1969).
Benedicti regula, ed. R. Hanslik, *CSEL* 75 (1960).
Two lives of St Cuthbert, ed. B. Colgrave (Cambridge, 1940).
Memorials of St Dunstan, ed. W. Stubbs, Rolls Ser. 63 (1874).
Gregory, *Liber responsalis*, Migne, *Patrologia latina* 78: 725–850.
     Liber sacramentorum, Migne, *Patrologia latina* 78: 25–264.
Felix's life of St Guthlac, ed. B. Colgrave (Cambridge, 1956).
Macrobius: Commentary on the Dream of Scipio, transl. W. H. Stahl (Columbia, 1952).
Regularis concordia, ed. T. Symons (London, 1953).
William of Malmesbury, *Gesta pontificum*, ed. N. E. S. A. Hamilton, Rolls Ser. 52 (1870).

3 Secondary works

For further references see *The new Cambridge Bibliography*, ed. G. Watson, I (1974), 187–356, and the annual bibliographies in *ASE* 1 (1972) onwards.

Andersson, T. M., *Early epic scenery: Homer, Virgil and the medieval legacy* (Ithaca, 1976).
Auerbach, E., *Literary language and its public*, transl. R. Manheim (London, 1965).
Baird, J. L., 'Unferth the *pyle*', *MÆ* 39 (1970), 1–12.
Barley, N. F., 'Old English colour classification: where do matters stand?', *ASE* 3 (1974), 15–28.

Birch, W. de Gray, *An ancient manuscript of the eighth or ninth century, formerly belonging to St Mary's Abbey or Nunnaminster*, Hampshire Record Soc. (1889).

Bliss, A. J., *The metre of Beowulf* (Oxford, 1958).
　　'Single half-lines in Old English poetry', *N & Q* 216 (1971), 442–9.

Bollard, J. K., 'The Cotton Maxims', *Neophilologus* 57 (1973), 179–81.

Bolton, W. F., 'Boethius, Alfred and *Deor* again', *MP* 69 (1971–72), 222–27.

Bonjour, A., *The digressions in Beowulf* (Oxford, 1950).
　　Twelve Beowulf papers (Neuchâtel, 1962).

Bonner, J. H., 'Towards a unified critical approach to Old English poetic composition', *MP* 73 (1975–76), 219–28.

Bright, J. W., 'The relation of the Caedmonian *Exodus* to the liturgy', *MLN* 27 (1912), 97–103.

Brodeur, A. G., *The art of Beowulf* (Berkeley, 1959).

Bruce-Mitford, R., *Aspects of Anglo-Saxon archaeology* (London, 1974).
　　The Sutton Hoo ship burial I, British Museum Publications (London, 1975).
—— and M. Bruce-Mitford, 'The Sutton Hoo lyre, *Beowulf*, and the origins of the frame harp', *Antiquity* 44 (1970), 7–13.

Burlin, R. B. and Irving, E. B., *Old English Studies in honour of John C. Pope* (Toronto, 1974).

Cable, T., 'Rules for syntax and metrics in *Beowulf*', *JEGP* 69 (1970), 81–8.
　　The meter and melody of Beowulf (Illinois, 1974).
　　'Parallels to the melodic formulas of *Beowulf*', *MP* 73 (1975–76), 1–14.

Calder, D. G., 'Setting and mode in *The seafarer* and *The wanderer*', *NM* 72 (1971), 264–75.
　　'Perspective and movement in *The ruin*', *NM* 72 (1971), 442–5.
　　'The vision of paradise: a symbolic reading of "The phoenix"', *ASE* 1 (1972), 167–81.
—— and M. J. B. Allen, *Sources and analogues of Old English poetry* (Cambridge, 1976).

Campbell, J. J., 'Learned rhetoric in Old English poetry', *MP* 63 (1965–66), 189–201.
　　'Knowledge of rhetorical figures in Anglo-Saxon England', *JEGP* 66 (1967), 1–20.

Chambers, R. W., *Beowulf: An introduction*, 3rd ed. (Cambridge, 1959).

Clemoes, P., *Rhythm and cosmic order in Old English Christian literature* (Cambridge, 1970).

Cross, J. E., ' "Ubi sunt" passages in Old English—sources and relationships', *Vetenskaps-Societens i Lund Årsbok* (1956), 25–44.
　　'On *The Wanderer* lines 80–84, a study of a figure and a theme', *Vetenskaps-Societetens i Lund Årsbok* (1958–9), 77–110.

'On the genre of *The wanderer*', *Neophilologus* 45 (1961), 63–75.

'The Old English poetic theme of "The gifts of men"', *Neophilologus* 46 (1962), 60–70.

'The literate Anglo-Saxon: on sources and disseminations', *Gollancz Memorial lecture, Proc. Brit. Acad.* 58 (1972), 67–100.

Daunt, M., 'Minor realism and contrast in *Beowulf*', *Mélanges de linguistique et de philologie: Fernand Mossé in memoriam*, ed. J. Vendryes (Paris, 1959), 87–94.

'Some modes of Anglo-Saxon meaning', *In Memory of J. R. Firth*, ed. C. E. Bazell *et al.* (London, 1966), 66–78.

Dawson, R. M., 'The structure of the Old English gnomic poems', *JEGP* 61 (1962), 14–22.

Doubleday, J. F., '*The ruin*: structure and theme', *JEGP* 71 (1972), 369–81.

Elliott, R. W. V., 'Cynewulf's runes in *Christ II* and *Elene*', *English Studies* 34 (1953), 49–57.

'Cynewulf's runes in *Juliana* and *Fates of the apostles*', *English Studies* 34 (1953), 193–204.

Fleming, J. V., '*The dream of the rood* and Anglo-Saxon monasticism', *Traditio* 22 (1966), 43–72.

Frankis, P. J., '*Deor* and *Wulf and Eadwacer*: some conjectures', *MÆ* 31 (1962), 161–75.

'The thematic significance of *enta geweorc* and related imagery in *The wanderer*', *ASE* 2 (1973), 253–69.

Fukuchi, M. S., 'Gnomic statements in Old English poetry', *Neophilologus* 59 (1975), 610–13.

Gatch, M. McC., *Loyalties and traditions: man and his world in Old English literature* (New York, 1971).

Goldsmith, M., *The mode and meaning of Beowulf* (London, 1970).

Green, D. H., *The Carolingian lord* (Cambridge, 1965).

Greenfield, S. B., 'The formulaic expression of the theme of "exile" in Anglo-Saxon poetry', *Speculum* 30 (1955), 200–206.

A critical history of Old English literature (New York, 1965).

The interpretation of Old English poems (London, 1972).

'The authenticating voice in *Beowulf*', *ASE* 5 (1976), 51–62.

Halliday, M. A. K., McIntosh, A. and Strevens, P., *The linguistic sciences and language teaching* (London, 1964).

Heimann, A., 'Three illustrations from the Bury St Edmunds Psalter and their prototypes', *Journal of the Warburg and Courtauld Institutes* 29 (1966), 39–59.

Henry, P. L., *The early English and Celtic lyric* (London, 1966).

Hieatt, C. B., 'Dream frame and verbal echo in *The dream of the rood*', *NM* 72 (1971), 251–63.

Hill, T. D., 'Notes on the Old English *Maxims I* and *II*', *N & Q* 215 (1970), 445–7.

Hume, K., 'The concept of the hall in Old English poetry', *ASE* 3 (1974), 63–74.

'The theme and structure of *Beowulf*', *SP* 72 (1975), 1–27.

'The "Ruin motif" in Old English poetry', *Anglia* 94 (1976), 339–60.

Huppé, B. F., *Doctrine and poetry: Augustine's influence on Old English poetry* (New York, 1959).

John, E., '*Beowulf* and the margins of literacy', *Bull. John Rylands Univ. Library* 56 (1974), 388–422.

Jones, C. W., *Bedae Opera de temporibus* (Cambridge, Mass., 1943).

Jones, G., *Kings, beasts and heroes* (London, 1972).

Kaske, R. E., '*Sapientia et fortitudo* as the controlling theme of *Beowulf*', *SP* 55 (1958), 423–56.

Leclercq, J., 'Études sur le vocabulaire monastique du moyen âge', *Studia Anselmiana* 48 (1961).

'Études sur le vocabulaire de la contemplation au moyen âge', *Studia Anselmiana* 51 (1963).

Lee, A. T., '*The ruin*: Bath or Babylon?', *NM* 74 (1973), 443–55.

Lee, N. A., 'The unity of *The dream of the rood*', *Neophilologus* 56 (1972), 469–86.

Logeman, H., 'Anglo-Saxonica minora', *Anglia* 11 (1888), 97–120, and 12 (1889), 497–518.

McIntosh, A., 'Wulfstan's prose', *Gollancz Memorial lecture*, *Proc. Brit. Acad.* 35 (1949), 109–42.

Magoun, F. P., 'The theme of the beasts of battle in Anglo-Saxon poetry', *NM* 56 (1955), 81–90.

Malone, K., 'Gnomic poem B of the Exeter Book', *MÆ* 12 (1943), 65–7.

Markland, M. F., 'Boethius, Alfred and *Deor*', *MP* 66 (1968–9), 1–4.

Murphy, J. J., *Rhetoric in the Middle Ages* (Berkeley, 1974).

Nicholson, L. E., and Frese, D. W., *Anglo-Saxon poetry: essays in appreciation* (Notre Dame, 1975).

Ogilvy, J. D. A., *Books known to the English 597–1066* (Cambridge, Mass., 1967).

Pope, J. C., *The rhythm of Beowulf* (New Haven, 1942, rev. 1966).

Raw, B., '*The dream of the rood* and its connections with early Christian art', *MÆ* 39 (1970), 239–56.

Reynolds, R., 'An echo of *Beowulf* in Athelstan's charters of 931–933 A.D.?', *MÆ* 24 (1955), 101–3.

Schedler, M., *Die Philosophie des Macrobius und ihr Einfluss auf die Wissenschaft des Christlichen Mittelalters, Beitr. zur Geschichte der Philosophie des Mittelalters, Texte und Untersuchungen*, Bd xiii, Heft 1 (1916).

Shepherd, G., 'The prophetic Cædmon', *RES NS* 5 (1954), 113–22.

'Scriptural poetry', *Continuations and beginnings*, ed. E. G. Stanley (London, 1966), 1–36.

'The nature of alliterative poetry in late Medieval England', *Gollancz Memorial lecture*, *Proc. Brit. Acad.* 56 (1970), 57–76.

Shippey, T. A., *Old English verse* (London, 1972).
  Poems of wisdom and learning in Old English (Cambridge, 1976).
Short, D. D., 'Leoðocræftas and the Pauline analogy of the body in the Old English *Gifts of men*', *Neophilologus* 59 (1975), 463–5.
Sievers, E., 'Zur Rhythmik des germanischen Alliterationsverses I', *Beitr. zur Geschichte der deutschen Sprache und Literatur* 10 (1885), 209–314.
  Altgermanische Metrik (Halle, 1893).
Sisam, K., *Studies in the history of Old English literature* (Oxford, 1953).
  'Anglo-Saxon royal genealogies', *Proc. Brit. Acad.* 39 (1953), 287–348.
  The structure of Beowulf (Oxford, 1965).
Smithers, G. V., 'The meaning of *The seafarer* and *The wanderer*', *MÆ* 26 (1957), 137–53, and 28 (1959), 99–106.
  The making of Beowulf (Durham, 1962).
Stanley, E. G., 'Old English poetic diction and the interpretation of *The wanderer, The seafarer* and *The penitent's prayer*', *Anglia* 73 (1955), 413–66.
  Continuations and beginnings: Studies in Old English literature (London, 1966).
Storms, G., 'The subjectivity of the style of *Beowulf*', *Studies in Old English literature in honor of A. G. Brodeur*, ed. S. B. Greenfield (Eugene, Oregon, 1963), 171–86.
Thorndike, L., *A history of magic and experimental science* (New York, 1923).
Thornley, G. C., 'The accents and points of MS Junius 11', *Trans. Phil. Soc.* (1954), 178–205.
Tolkein, J. R. R., 'Beowulf: the monsters and the critics', *Gollancz Memorial lecture, Proc. Brit. Acad.* 22 (1936), 245–95.
Waddilove, W., 'Basic blacksmithing: part 3, heat treatment', *Practical Self-sufficiency* 6 (October–November 1976), 26–8.
Whitelock, D., 'The interpretation of *The seafarer*', *The early cultures of north-west Europe*, ed. C. Fox and B. Dickins (Cambridge, 1950), 259–72.
  The audience of Beowulf (Oxford, 1957).
Wilson, R. M., *The lost literature of medieval England* (London, 1952).
Woolf, R., 'The ideal of men dying with their lord in the *Germania* and in *The battle of Maldon*', *ASE* 5 (1976), 63–81.
Wormald, F., *English drawings of the tenth and eleventh centuries* (London, 1952).
  'An English eleventh-century psalter with pictures', *Walpole Society* 38 (1962), 1–13.
Wrenn, C. L., 'The poetry of Cædmon', *Gollancz Memorial lecture, Proc. Brit. Acad.* 32 (1946), 277–95.
  A study of Old English literature (London, 1967).
Wright, D. H., *The Vespasian psalter*, EEMF (1967).

Index

Abraham 1, 54, 84; battle of the kings 36, 82
acrobats 12, 73
Adam and Eve 82; Christ the second Adam 129
advent antiphons 39–40
Ælfric, homilist (d. *circa* 1010) 2, 12, 16
Æschere, thane of Hrothgar 101, 111
Æthelweard, patron of Ælfric 2
Alcuin of York (d. 804) 3, 9, 29
Aldhelm of Malmesbury (d. 709) 3, 12, 29
Alfred, king of Wessex (d. 899) 9, 11; Boethius 25, 28; *Cura Pastoralis* 4
allegory 2, 9, 37, 54, 127; *see also* metaphor; symbolism
alliteration 5, 14–16, 97, 99; *see also* metre
Andreas 2, 5, 51, 59; formulaic opening 35, 114
Anglo-Saxon Chronicle 17, 74; poems of 2–3, 11, 16–17, 20, 30–31; rhythmic prose 16
animals and birds 48–9, 54–9, 73–4, 79, 82; *see also* beasts of battle
anonymity 6, 8
archaism 4, 65
armour 32–3, 35, 58, 83, 92–4
Asser's Life of King Alfred 11
Athelstan, king of Wessex (d. 939) charter of 9; Brunanburh 16, 46

audience 8–10, 31–5, 38, 39–43, 86, 91–2, 123, 128; co-creator of the poem 68–9, 74–5, 81; shared experience 30–31, 85, 115
Augustine of Hippo (d. 430), *De doctrina Christiana* 16; theory of style 117; vocabulary of prayer 129
authenticating phrases 30–33, 35–8, 40, 42–3, 82, 93
authorial presence 31–5, 40–44, 85; *see also* poetic authority
Azarias 2, 7

Battle of Brunanburh 16, 46; authenticating phrases 31; beasts of battle 55–6
Battle of Maldon 11, 23, 46; and *Genesis A* 82; authenticating phrases 30–31; date 4; landscape 49; manuscript 3; rhythm 117, 119–20
battle of Nechtanesmere 128
beasts of battle 55–6, 74, 82, 117–19; *see also* animals and birds
Bede (d. 735) 3, 11; age of 8–9; Cædmon 3, 11–14, 19, 21; *Death song* 3, 6, 115; Macrobius 128
beginnings 6, 30, 31, 37–8, 85–7, 114–15
Belshazzar 17, 83
Beowulf 3, 8–9, 12, 17–19, 20–24, 37–8, 67, 84–96, 98–115, 117–18, 122; authorial presence 31–

5, 40; beasts of battle 56, 74; beginning 31, 85–7; cadences 100–101, 103–4, 106–7, 113; characterization, 47–8, 89–90, 112–13; colour and light 51–2; date 4, 8; descriptive techniques 58–60; digressions 89, 90, 93–6; divine and natural order 61–3, 77–8; ending 87–8; entertainment 11–12, 17–19, 26, 28; Frisian expedition 93–5; generalized comment 33–5, 44, 75; historical material 95–6; landscape 48–50, 63, 67; manuscript 1, 2, 4; messenger 27, 56, 88, 95; metre and rhythm 98–115; music 23–9, 56; narrative technique 84–96; solitary survivor 26; structure 89; suspense 90–93; syntax 15–16, 98–100; theme 85–7, 95–6

Beowulf, son of Ecgtheow 17–18, 20–24, 26–8, 32–4, 47–8, 58–9, 86–96, 101–3, 106–14; and Beowulf the Dane 34; and Grendel 17, 33, 86, 89, 90, 92–3, 101, 106; and Grendel's mother 33, 89, 92, 107; and Hrothgar 23–4, 32; and Hygelac 23, 26, 93–5; and Widsith 13; as hero 95–6; as king 94; character 47–8, 87–90, 95–6, 113; death 27–8, 86–8, 95; dragon fight 22, 33, 35, 48, 49, 52, 58–9, 88, 89, 93–5; funeral 32–3, 58; reminiscences 18, 26; speech patterns 108–14; strength 33; youth 93

Beowulf, son of Scyld 34, 86, 87

Bible, Gen. i–xxii 12 82; Exod. xi 4–5 131; xiii–xiv 83; Job xi 7–9 124; Ps. viii 70; Song of Songs v 2 131; Ecclus xliv 1–9 70; Wisdom xviii 14–15 131; Matt.

xxiv 42–44 131; xxv 14–30 70; xxv 34–45 41; Luke ii 38; xxiv 26 130; John xxi 24 37; ix 4 79; Rom. xii 3–8 69; Ephes. iii 14–21 124; iv 7–12 24, 69

biblical paraphrase 35–7, 82–5
birds *see* animals and birds
Bliss, A.J. 97, 108–9
blood-feud 9; *see also* heroic ideal
Boethius, *Consolation of Philosophy* 17, 19, 25, 28, 61, 67; *Cotton metres* 14–15
Breca 58
Breviary readings 1–2, 84; *see also* liturgy
Brosings, necklace of 93
Byrhtferth's Manual 67, 128
Byrhtnoth 9, 46, 82; *see also Battle of Maldon*

Cable, T. 97, 109
cadences 100–104, 106–107, 113
Cædmon (*c.*658–680) 3, 11–14, 19, 25, 131; *Hymn* 3, 6, 8, 21–2
Canons of Edgar 12
characterization 45–8, 65–7, 87–90, 95–6, 112–13, 116
Chaucer 1
Christ 1, 29, 38, 39, 41, 129–31; body of 69, 127; king handing out gifts 24, 69; the second Adam 129
Christ I 2, 5, 30, 39–40, 62, 123
Christ II 2, 6, 19, 24–5, 29, 30, 40–41, 69, 115, 121–2, 127; *see also* Cynewulf
Christ III 2, 41, 53, 59, 79, 115
Christ and Satan 1, 5, 29, 61, 115
Christopher, homily on 2
church, influence of 3
classification of styles and themes 11, 16–17, 116–17
colour and light 49, 51–5; *brun* 52; *fealo* 52–3, 55; *grene* 53–4; *har* 49, 53; *read* 53; *sweart* 53–4

comitatus 9, 20, 22, 27, 33, 45, 46, 50, 82, 87–8; *see also* heroic ideal; retainership

consolation 25–6, 46, 66, 88

Constantine, emperor (d. 337) 38, 55, 117–18, 120; *see also Elene*

contemptus mundi 68–9, 127

contracted forms 4

contrast 29, 35, 47–8, 62, 71, 88–9, 91

convention 9–10, 30, 46, 47, 50–51, 53, 65–6, 74, 88, 117, 122

craftsmanship 62–4, 65; in poetry 10, 11, 13–14

critical problems 8–10

Cura Pastoralis, MS Hatton 20, 4

Cuthbert, bishop of Lindisfarne (d. 687) 4, 128

Cynewulf 6–7, 19, 24–5, 29, 30; poetic authority 38, 40–41; rhythm 115–22; signature 6–7; symbolism 62; views on poetry 24–5; *see also Christ II*; *Elene*; *Fates of the apostles*; *Juliana*

Dæghrefn, the Frankish champion 94–5

Danes 4, 21, 31, 85, 89–91, 94

Daniel 1, 17, 83–4; and *Azarias* 2, 7; poetic authority 35–7

date of poems 4, 8–9

David 24

death 26–8, 34, 56, 66–9, 73–5, 78, 86–7, 94–5, 126–7, 129–32; as sleep 68, 129–32

Deor 3, 12–13, 42–3

descriptive techniques 48–60; colour 49, 51–5; generalization 45–51; light effects 51–2; movement 58–9; pattern 60–62; sound effects 59; technical detail 59–60

devil 1, 29, 83; as thief 127

digressions 10, 85, 89–95; function of 95–6

divine and natural order 48–9, 60–62, 64, 70, 73, 75–80

dragons, habitat 45, 48–9; movement 58–9; nature 33; resentment 35; *see also* Beowulf, son of Ecgtheow

Dream of the rood 2, 5; opening line 114; poetic authority 36, 41–3; prayer 123, 127–32; two texts 7–8

dreams, classification of 128

Dryhtelm, vision of 128

Dunstan, archbishop of Canterbury (d. 988) 3, 29

Durham 4

Eadgils, Swedish king, son of Ohthere, brother of Eanmund 95

Eadgils, lord of Widsith, ruler of the Myrgings 13, 44

Ealhhild, daughter of Eadwine, wife of Eormanric, patron of Widsith 20, 44, 47

Eanmund, son of Ohthere, brother of Eadgils, killed by Weohstan 95

Ecgfrith, king of Northumbria (d. 685) 128

Ecgtheow, father of Beowulf 89

Edgar, king of England (d. 975), poems on 16, 31

Edwin, king of Northumbria (d. 632) 128

Egyptians 83–4, 119, 131

Elam, king of 82

elegy 2, 18, 26–7, 43, 66–9

Elene 2, 4–6, 25; authenticating phrases 38; beasts of battle 55; beginning 38, 85, 115; characterization 46, 116; date 4; ending 5; rhythm 115–21; *see also* Cynewulf

Elphinston, John 3
encomiastic verse 19–23, 126
endings 5, 10, 87–9
entertainment 10, 11–12, 18–19, 26–8, 30, 56
Eormanric, king of the Goths (d. circa 375) 3, 13, 19, 43–4, 65
eschatology 41, 68, 72, 79, 128–32
exemplary figures 45–8, 65–9; *see also* characterization
Exhortation to Christian living 30
exile 44, 45, 56, 66, 126–7, 132
Exodus 1, 4, 51, 83–5, 114; beasts of battle 55, 118–19; poetic authority 35–7; purpose 83–5; structure 83
expectations, creation of 9–10, 85–7, 91–3

fame *see* reputation
Fates of the apostles 2, 5–6, 25, 69, 115; *see also* Cynewulf
fictive speaker 18, 42–4, 65–6, 68
Fight at Finnsburg 3, 51–2; tale of 18, 90, 93, 96
formulae 5, 9, 22, 35, 38, 43, 46, 50, 82–3, 114–15, 119; *see also* authenticating phrases
Fortunes of men 12, 67, 69, 73–4; *see also* gnomic poetry
Franks 93
Freawaru, daughter of Hrothgar 47, 93, 96
friendship 79–80
Frisian expedition 93–5

Geats 85, 88, 90, 93, 94, 96
genealogies 9
generalizations 33–5, 44, 75, 79, 101; exemplary figures 45–8; landscape 48–51; *see also* gnomic poetry
generosity 19–20, 32, 34, 44, 85–7, 96; *see also* heroic ideal

Genesis A 1, 82–4, 115; authenticating phrases 36, 82; colour and light 51, 53–4; *see also* manuscripts, Junius 11
Genesis B 4, 82–3; colour words 53
gifts of God 24–5, 69–73
Gifts of men 12, 19, 77; genre 69–70; structure 69, 71–3; syntax 67; *see also* gnomic poetry
gnomic poetry 2, 11–12, 17–18, 23–6, 33, 44, 45, 47–9, 61, 75; *see also Fortunes of men*; *Gifts of men*; *Maxims I* and *II*
God 25, 27, 34, 41–3, 54, 60–64, 69–80, 83, 86, 89, 123–6, 129, 131–2; as doctor 123; covenant with Abraham 84; gifts of 24–5, 69–73; redemptive plan 84; titles 21–2, 125–6; *see also* Christ
Grendel 17, 28–9, 32–5, 48–9, 62, 86–94, 97, 101–7, 114; ancestry 28–9, 89, 92; death 17, 32, 49, 86, 91–3; fight with 33–4, 59, 89–94, 101–7; head 107, 114
Grendel's mother 32–5, 48, 89–93, 103–107; attack on Heorot 35, 91–3, 103; death 32; emotions 35; fight with 33, 89, 92, 107; tracks 58
Guthlac A 2, 23, 29, 37, 54, 57
Guthlac B 2, 29, 37
Guthlac, Latin life of 23, 37

Hæthcyn, son of Hrethel and brother of Hygelac 26
hall 19, 28, 45, 76, 80, 86–7; *see also* Heorot
Hama 101
harmony and disharmony 29
harps 11–12, 18–19, 23–4, 28–9; *see also* music
Healfdene, father of Hrothgar 32, 34

Heardred, son of Hygelac, and cousin of Beowulf 21, 48, 95

heaven 29, 76, 126–32

hell 29, 128

Heorogar, elder brother of Hrothgar 32

Heorot 18, 28, 32–3, 35, 59, 62, 85–6, 89, 93–4, 110; *see also* hall

Herebeald, son of Hrethel and brother of Hygelac 26

Heremod, king of the Danes 96, 101

heroes 3, 20–23, 43–4, 47–8, 85–6, 88–9, 113

heroic and unheroic images 74

heroic ideal 9, 23, 27, 34, 46, 74, 82, 87, 94; critique of 85, 87–8, 95–6; *see also* historical material; loyalty; nobility; retainership; tragedy; youth and age

heroic poetry 3, 9, 23, 36, 74, 85, 91; religious heroic 82–4

Hickes, George 3

Hildeburh, wife of Finn 47, 101

historical material 3, 11, 85, 88, 93–6

Homiletic fragment I 2

homiletic writing 2, 16–17, 41, 67–8, 83–5

Hondscio, companion of Beowulf 93, 105

Hrethel, king of the Geats and grandfather of Beowulf 26, 89, 93

Hrethric, son of Hrothgar 94

Hrothgar, king of the Danes 11, 13, 17–18, 21–8, 32–4, 47–9, 85–6, 89–96, 101, 103, 109–14; and Beowulf 89–96, 109–14; building of Heorot 28, 32–3, 85–6; court of 26, 28, 32, 90: generosity 32–3; *god cyning* 21, 96; playing the harp 11, 18, 23; wisdom 23–4, 47–8

Hrothmund, son of Hrothgar 94

Hrothulf, nephew of Hrothgar 94

Huns 117, 120

Husband's message 57–8

Hygd, wife of Hygelac 32

Hygelac, king of the Geats, uncle and lord of Beowulf 13, 23, 26, 32–3, 89, 93–6, 109–11; death 93–5; recklessness 46, 48, 86

imagery 26–8, 54–9, 62–4, 66–8, 74–6, 80, 126–7, 129–32

Ingeld, son-in-law of Hrothgar 3

inspiration 10, 11, 13, 25, 65, 82; *see also* tradition

interpretation of poems 8–10, 97

irony 91, 94

Isaac 84

Isaiah 40

Israelites 83–4, 119

Jacob 84

Jerusalem 39–40, 83–4

judgment 40–41, 68, 71–2, 128, 130

Judgment day II 53, 115

Judith 2, 46, 55, 118–19

Juliana 2, 5–7, 46–7, 62, 114–17; beginning 38, 114–15; characterization 46–7, 116; rhythm 114–17; runic signature 6–7; *see also* Cynewulf

kingship 19–24, 45, 47–8, 85–9, 94–6

Lactantius, *Carmen de ave phoenice* 37, 54

lament for the past 26–7, 66–9

landscape 48–52, 54–5, 62–4, 67–8; *see also* descriptive techniques

language 7, 9, 13–17, 123, 129; levels of 109–17; *see also* literary dialect; metaphor; rhetoric; style; syntax, word-play

Letter of Alexander to Aristotle 2
libraries, Bodleian 3; Cotton 3; dispersal of medieval libraries 3; Lambeth Palace 3; medieval catalogues 3–4; Vatican 4
life as a loan 75–7
light and dark 28, 39, 51–2, 62, 86–7
Lindisfarne 3
lists 3, 22, 43–4, 65, 69–74
literary dialect 4
liturgy 1, 39–41, 84; Good Friday 41; *see also* Breviary readings; prayer
Lot 36, 82
loyalty 9, 23, 80, 85–7, 90, 94–6; *see also* heroic ideal

Macrobius, *Commentary on the dream of Scipio* 128
Mainz 4
manuscripts 1–7, 24, 30, 67 n, 79 n, 82–4; appearance 5; contents 1–3; loss of 3–4; illustrations 1, 2, 24, 67 n2, 79 n13; numbered sections 1, 5, 83–4; specific manuscripts: *Beowulf* MS 1–4; Exeter book 1–7; Hatton 20 4; Julius A ii 30; Junius 11 1–2, 5, 82–4; Lambeth Palace 427 30; Vercelli book 1–2, 5–7
Marvels of the East 2
Mary 39–40
Maxims I (Exeter maxims) 60–63, 74–80; categories of men and women 45, 47; consolation of music 26; genre 69, 74–5; jewels 63; order 60–61, 76–7; structure 75–80; wisdom 18, 24, 30, 74; wolves 49, 74; *see also* gnomic poetry
Maxims II (Cotton maxims) 34, 48–9, 73–4; categories of men 45; genre 69; kingship 48;

monsters 48–9; order 61, 73; *see also* gnomic poetry
meditation 10, 39, 123, 128–32; *see also* prayer
Menologion 63
Merovingians 27, 88
metaphor 16, 19, 62–3, 126–7, 132; *see also* allegory
metre and rhythm 5, 14–16, 65, 79, 97–122, 124; *see also* Bliss; Cable; Pope; Sievers
minstrels 12–13, 19–20, 22–23, 29, 33, 43–4, 93
models for behaviour 23
monasteries 3, 9–10
Moses 35–6, 83–4
movement 58–9
music 11–13, 18–19, 23–9; symbolism 28–9

narrative technique 82–96
nature 48, 55, 60–64, 77–8; art 55, 63–4; seasons 61, 77–8; symbolism 62; *see also* divine and natural order
Nebuchadnezzar 83
Noah 1, 35, 54, 84
nobility 85–6; *see also* heroic ideal

Odda, sons of 46
Odinn 78
Offa, king of Angel 33
Offa, king of Mercia (d. 796) 8
old age and the dying world 68, 75
Old Saxon *Genesis* 4, 82; *see also Genesis B*
Onela, king of Sweden 32–3, 95
Ongentheow, king of Sweden, father of Onela 33, 48
oral tradition *see* tradition
Order of the world 30, 67, 73
originality *see* inspiration

parallelism 91–3, 117–18, 120–22, 123–6

Partridge 5
Pater noster, Credo, Gloria 123
patronage 7, 19–20, 23, 43–4
pattern 60–62, 118, 121, 124, 132
Paul, apostle 69, 124
performance 6, 10, 19, 97–8, 108–9; *see also* expectations; metre; music
Pharaoh 55
Phoenix 2, 5, 63, 115; authenticating phrases 37; colour symbolism 54–5
poetic authority 30–44, 69; books 35–8, 40–41, 65, 115; tradition 31–3, 65; personal knowledge 30–33; impersonation 41–4; shared experience 31–5, 40, 43, 45, 115; figure of authority 40–42; *see also* authenticating phrases
poetic form 10, 65–81, 82–4, 89, 92, 123, 127–9; theory of 16–17; words for 17–19; implicit and explicit 69; *see also* audience; beginnings; endings; lists; variation
poetic language 13, 16
poetic technique 9–10, 11–29, 122; contrast 71, 88–89; variation 89–93, 118–22; *see also* metre; vocabulary
poetry, curative power 25–6; functions 19–26; pattern for behaviour 23; praise 19–23; preservation of wisdom 23–5; prophecy 25; recording the past 23; survival of 3–4; symbolism 26; themes 11
poets, authority 30–44, 65, 81; functions 19–26, 45; names 3, 6–7, 11; signatures 6–7; status 11–13; rewards 7, 13, 44; *see also* Alcuin; Aldhelm; Bede; Cædmon; Cynewulf; *Deor*; minstrels; patronage; *Widsith*

Pope, J. C. 97
popular songs 3, 13
praise of kings and heroes 19–23
Prayer (Julius A.ii) 30, 123–6, 132
prayer 7, 11, 30, 123–32; for the dying 84; language of 129; *see also* meditation
Precepts 42, 69
Preface of the Mass 21
private reading 10, 30, 97, 123
prose and verse, distinction between 5, 11, 14–18, 116–17
proverbial material 11, 69
public recitation 10, 30
punctuation 5

quotation 65–9, 119–21

reading aloud 5, 10
realism 33–4, 58–9
Red Sea 1, 83–4
reputation 9, 19–23, 44, 90; *see also* heroic ideal
Resignation 30, 123, 126–7, 130–32
retainership 27, 34, 45–6, 87–8, 94–5; *see also comitatus*
reward 7; *see also* heroic ideal
rhetoric 16, 85, 121–2, 124–5, 132
rhyme 121
rhythm *see* metre
rhythmic prose 14, 16–17
Riddles 2, 17 (no. 8), 51 (nos. 1–3), 53 n8 (nos. 11, 48), 59 n15 (no. 58), 60
Ruin 53, 60
Rune poem 69
runic signatures 6–7; *see also* Cynewulf
Ruthwell cross 7–8

saints' lives 2, 23, 82
Sarah, wife of Abraham 46
Satan *see* devil

Scyld, king of the Danes, *god cyning* 21, 96, 99; funeral 32–3, 86, 100; power 82, 85–6, 99

Seafarer 2, 5, 27, 42–3, 57, 65, 67–9, 115, 123–4; fictive speaker 42–3; genre 18; symbolism 127; syntax 123–4; theme 68–9; universality 46, 75; weather 68

sea imagery 76, 127

seasons 61, 77–8

Seasons for fasting 11

set-piece descriptions 65, 67, 91, 117, 119, 121

Sievers, E. 15, 97–8

Sigemund 3, 49, 90

singing 12–13, 18–19, 23–6, 29

sleep *see* death

Sodom and Gomorrah 54, 82

Solomon and Saturn 3, 42, 60–61, 68–9, 81, 115; prose version 67

Soul and body I 2, 7, 30, 74

sound effects 59; *see also* music

speaker *see* fictive speaker; poetic authority

speech rhythms 102–103, 108–16

structure *see* poetic form

style, theory of 16–17, 116–17, 122; *sermo humilis*, 117; style of discourse 112; *see also* language; metre and rhythm

Sutton Hoo 11

Swedes 27, 85, 88, 95–6

symbolism 9, 53–4, 62, 76, 80; *see also* allegory; metaphor

Symeon of Durham, *Historia Dunelmensis ecclesiae* 4

syntax 14–17, 39, 67, 71–3, 98–100, 116, 118, 120–22, 123–6, 132; *see also* metre and rhythm

Taplow 11

technical detail 59–60

texts, changes in 7–8; date 4, 8; status of 6–8

themes, classification of 16–17, 116–17

Theodoric, son of Clovis, king at Rheims 511–34 43

titles of kings 22, 126

titles of poems 5

tradition 5–10, 31–3, 35–8, 65–6, 122; bookish 35–8, 40, 65; oral 3, 5–6, 8, 35, 65; shared 31–3, 35, 45, 66, 81; *see also* inspiration; poetic authority; quotation; set-piece descriptions

tragedy 85–6, 95–6

transience 23, 26–7, 66–9, 70, 86–7

treasure 26, 32–3, 76–7, 88, 93

trumpets 19, 29, 59, 118

þula, þyle 23, 94

Unferth 89, 94, 107, 112–14; speech patterns 112–13; status 23

Vainglory 5, 30, 114

variation 17, 89–93, 122, 123–6

visions 42, 127–9

vocabulary 14, 16, 65–8, 82, 116, 127; of prayer 129; *see also* formulae

Wægmundings 95

Waldere 3

Wanderer 2, 26–7, 42–3, 45–6, 65–8, 115; beasts of battle 56; exile 45–6; form 65–8; landscape 48; transience 26–7

Wealhtheow, wife of Hrothgar 17, 32, 47, 91, 93–4, 111

weapons *see* armour

weather 48, 57, 62, 67–8

Weland 3, 67

Whitby 6, 11

Widsith 3, 11, 13, 19–20, 22–3, 35, 43–4, 65; impersonation

Widsith (continued)
43–4, 65; performance 19;
praise of kings 22; status of
poets 13
Wife's Lament 18, 42–3, 50–51
Wiglaf, son of Weohstan 33, 48,
87–8, 95, 112
William of Malmesbury 3
wisdom 17–18, 20, 24–7, 30, 45,
47, 67–9, 75, 78–9, 81
word-play 39, 77, 80
words and phrases specially mentioned: *bec cweðaþ, bec secgaþ* 36;
cræft 13; *dagas sind gewitene* 68;
deman 72, 77; *dom* 20, 72; *gedræg*
29; *dream* 18–19, 28; *dryhten* 22;
eardstapa 67; *ellengæst* 87; *elþe-
odigra eard* 69; *fæstnung* 66; *frea*
22; *fus ond fæge* 91, 127; *galan*
17; *gamen* 28; *gidd, giddian*
17–19, 25; *gleaw hæle* 67; *geglenced* 14; *gleo* 18–19; *gleoman* 12;
gliwian 12, 17; *god cyning* 21,
96; *hraþe* 90; *hwæt* 113–15; *hyht*
69; *ic beheold* 42; *ic gefrægn* 6,
30, 32, 35–7, 82; *ic gehyrde*
30–33; *ic geseah* 30, 36, 42; *læne*
75; *lean* 77, 79; *leoð* 17–19, 25;
lof 20, 87; *maðelode* 17; *metod* 22,
79; *mine gefræge* 30–31, 82; *oferhygd* 83; *onetteð* 68, 79–80;
otium 129; *quies* 129; *reccean* 19;
sabbatum 129; *sang* 17–19; *scop*
12–13, 23, 35, 43; *scyppend* 22;
secgan 17–19; *singan* 17–19, 25;
sona 90; *spell* 17–19; *sum* 66–7,
120–21; *swa heo no wære* 67;
swefn 131; *treo, treow* 80; *þyle* 23;
vacatio 129; *weard* 22; *we geas-
codon* 43; *we gefrunon* 31, 35, 38,
40, 43; *we hyrdon* 31, 38, 40; *wel
geworht* 14; *we þæt soð magon
secgan* 82; *wordum wrixlan*
17; *wrecan* 19; *wyrd* 61, 101
Wulf and Eadwacer 42–3
Wulf and Eofor 48
Wulfgar 22, 89, 109–10
Wulfstan, homilist (bishop of
Worcester 1003–1016, archbishop of York 1003–23) 16,
41
youth and age 24, 34, 47–8, 86–8